Learning with colleagues

Learning with colleagues

An action guide for peer consultation

Erik de Haan

Translated from the Dutch by Sue Stewart

Illustrations by Selma van Vemde

First published 2001 in the Netherlands as *Leren Met Collega's*

This edition published 2005 by
PALGRAVE MACMILLAN
Houndmills, Basingstoke, Hampshire RG21 6XS and
175 Fifth Avenue, New York, N.Y. 10010
Companies and representatives throughout the world

PALGRAVE MACMILLAN is the global academic imprint of the Palgrave
Macmillan division of St. Martin's Press, LLC and of Palgrave Macmillan Ltd.
Macmillan® is a registered trademark in the United States, United Kingdom and
other countries. Palgrave is a registered trademark in the European Union and
other countries.

ISBN 1-4039-4287-0

This book is printed on paper suitable for recycling and made from fully
managed and sustained forest sources.

A catalogue record for this book is available
from the British Library.

A catalog record for this book is available
from the Library of Congress.

10 9 8 7 6 5 4 3 2 1
14 13 12 11 10 09 08 07 06 05

Printed and bound in China

To Carmen for sharing
so much of the learning

Contents

Figures and tables

Figures

Tables

Preface

The era of learning with colleagues

A book about learning with colleagues is entirely in keeping with the spirit of our times. Both the nature and role of 'work' have changed radically in the West in recent decades. Where we work can no longer be predicted on the basis of family background and education. How we work changes almost from month to month, if only due to new developments in the field of information and communications technology. What we expect from work is no longer clear either: for most of us, it is not just about earning a living. Work now serves other purposes, for example satisfying our more personal needs (Maslow, 1962) such as recognition, influence, self-expression and self-fulfilment. As a result, we now expect more and more from work and, by the same token, work has come to 'expect' more of us. Our working lives are gradually becoming more exciting and interesting. It is becoming increasingly difficult to take refuge behind unique expertise or customised approaches – instead, we now have to find a tailored solution for every job or client, to show more of our personal side in our work and to make that personal side 'effective'. 'Work' is becoming more like 'school', in two respects:

- In the contemporary sense of school: a place of training and education, a learning environment or independent study centre. A place we go to seeking self-development and self-fulfilment.
- In the original sense of the Greek *scholè*: leisure, rest, pleasure and, paradoxically enough, free time and ease. A place we go to find ourselves, to reflect and to spend time doing things that really matter to us.

Not surprisingly, many people find that the boundaries between the work and private spheres are becoming blurred, and increasing numbers of us feel we are more our 'true selves' at work than we are at home. In line with the spirit of the times, we want to learn at work and are keen to embark upon training courses and personal development activities directly connected with our work. We feel a greater need to talk to colleagues about our personal development, and even to work with them towards that development.

That is the basis of *learning with colleagues*, which does not mean induction programmes, skills training or on-the-job training. Learning with colleagues goes much further than that and involves:

- entering into a deeper relationship with your colleagues in order to learn from them
- being vulnerable and openly discussing your strengths and weaknesses
- finding the limits of your expertise and exploring the territory beyond those limits together with your colleagues
- seeing this process of searching and exploration as an integral part of your work.

If you don't do this, how are you to stay 'professional' and what are you going to learn from as a professional? Textbooks, which are outdated almost as soon as they reach the shelves? Clients and customers, who themselves aren't sure what questions they want to ask you?

In my own view, *peer consultation* is an activity that fits in with both meanings of 'school' – the learning environment and the place of leisure. Of the numerous ways in which you can develop yourself as an individual, peer consultation has significant advantages. You share the benefits of consultation sessions with your colleagues, they can be held close to your own place of work and, in many ways, they can offer the peace and concentration that is so greatly needed for learning. This book therefore starts with an introduction to peer consultation as a way of learning with colleagues. Later on, Part IV introduces other forms of learning which establish a closer link with your own work and place greater responsibility for learning on your own shoulders.

The structure of this book

This book, *Learning with Colleagues*, consists of four parts. Part I, *Peer Consultation*, contains a brief introduction to peer supervision and action learning, and includes a range of methods for using this tool in your own practice. Part II, *Facilitation*, discusses the special role of the facilitator of peer consultation, concentrating on the aspects of learning that a facilitator can take into account and may sometimes need to create. Part III, *Learning From Experience*, contains a theoretical discussion on experiential learning, including a number of concepts and models. Finally, Part IV, *From Consultation Groups to Learning Networks*, contains a broader perspective on learning with colleagues, including introductions to a number of instruments and work methods which go beyond peer consultation and so require more of participants.

Reading this book may in itself prove a valuable learning process. This process is structured in a considered manner, using the well-known model developed by Kolb (1984):

1. *Readers who want to get down to work right away* will find a number of tools in Part I to help them get started quickly. A brief introduction to peer supervision and action learning (Chapter 1) is followed by a discussion of 15 consultation methods widely used in practice (Chapter 4) and an outline of the basic preconditions for successful consultation (Chapter 6).

2. *For readers who want to pause and reflect* on the value of peer consultation, and perhaps improve their own performance while learning with colleagues, Parts I and II contain guidelines on the art of 'intervention' (Chapter 2), 'asking questions' (Chapter 3), 'choice of method' (Chapter 5), and 'giving feedback' (Chapter 10).

   There are also opportunities to reflect on the role of the facilitator (Chapters 7 and 8), creating the conditions for mutual learning (Chapter 9) and handling difficult moments in consultation groups (Chapter 13).

3. *Experienced readers who want to immerse themselves in the relevant book learning* should ideally start with Chapter 11. The book learning is represented by an introduction to group dynamic processes in small groups (Chapters 11 and 12) and several chapters on learning models (Chapters 14 to 18).

4. Finally, *readers who are keen to apply new models* and so go beyond the consultation methods, which are slightly one-sided in some respects (see Chapter 19), and who want to apply the broader theoretical concepts about learning styles and 'meta-learning' from Part III, are referred to Part IV. This part focuses on applications of the concepts, in terms of 'short-cycle learning' (Chapter 20), 'project-based action learning' (Chapter 21) and 'self-managed learning and learning networks' (Chapter 22).

This book has a progressive structure, therefore: from getting started (*accommodation*), to reflecting on the experiences gained (*divergence*), to incorporating those experiences into theoretical models (*assimilation*) and to applying those models and preparing for new actions in the field of learning (*convergence*). Chapter 15 defines the terms 'accommodation', 'divergence', 'assimilation' and 'convergence' and introduces the accompanying cyclic learning model.

Because this book is intended to fit in with professional practice as closely as possible several concrete, practical examples are provided from my own experience of organising and facilitating learning with very diverse colleagues. One particular case of learning with colleagues – my own learning process during the writing of this book, which has taken over four years – has been worked out in detail. This example runs like a leit-motif through Parts III and IV, where the example is repeatedly related to the topics under discussion.

In recent years it has emerged that many professionals use *Learning with Colleagues* as a reference text when they want to learn and develop together in their work. As a truly comprehensive reference, however, it lacked a number of essential elements. These have now been incorporated into this second edition:

- Choosing a consultation method during a learning group session has now been made easier by an extra chapter devoted to the subject (Chapter 5). The choice has also been substantially broadened, by the addition of three new associative methods in Chapter 4 (the storytelling method, the hologram method and organisation constellations).
- Information has been added about the long-term development of consultation groups, mainly because it is noticeable that many consultation groups 'get stuck'. Sometimes this occurs right at the start when 'things don't get off the ground'; often it happens later on, for example when they get 'dull and predictable'. Experiences like these are entirely normal. All consultation groups have to deal with them and, in particular, it is possible to move beyond them by recognising and reflecting on the development phase. Recognisable patterns in group development are examined from the perspective of the learning group facilitator (Chapter 11).
- I acknowledge that I struggled too long with a description of 'peer pressure' and the struggle involved in learning, in a bid to give the first edition a flavour of this downside of learning. At the time I got no further than my own diary of the writing of this book. Now I have managed to arrive at a somewhat more systematic description of learners' experiences from the inside and to draw attention to group pressure during learning (Chapter 18). It is a rather uncomfortable story, especially compared with many optimistic stories of 'learning organisations' and 'communities of practice'. But it is the story which I myself believe is closer to the truth than more idealised narratives. In my view, the outlook becomes optimistic and promising only when professionals are able to face up to this downside and overcome it, if only to a limited extent and for a limited time. To this end, a number of suggestions drawn from practice are given.
- Finally, two new Appendices (Appendix E and F) include a summary of our recent quantitative outcome research on *Learning with Colleagues* (de Haan and de Ridder, 2003), and an example of a large-scale organisational application of peer consultation, inside the BBC.

The author as mouthpiece

Who is the author of this guide to learning with colleagues? A devisor of learning models? A writer of textbooks? Someone who has developed a great personal capacity to learn with colleagues? None of these people. He sees himself as simply an editor of work done by others, a 'mouthpiece' for methods and knowledge which are often as old as the discipline of learning itself.[1]

Only five of the 15 consultation methods were developed by myself (the brainpicking method, learning from success, the storytelling method, the hologram method and organisation constellations) and my comments on giving feedback, asking questions, group dynamics, self-managed learning and other matters involve little original thought. That is why source references are included as much as possible, in order to acknowledge the authors who actually invented the concepts and methods discussed.

During the writing process I myself was busy learning, both alone, and from and with colleagues. Sections of this book have been discussed in a range of fora, and multiple versions have been read by various colleagues and clients with whom I have been using Parts I and II for many years. I would like to thank a number of my colleagues at this point. First of all, Ina Ahuis, Adrie van den Berge, Heleen Bruining and Willem Verheul (De Galan and Voigt, Amsterdam), without whom this book would never have come about. Heleen and Adrie wrote initial versions of most of the chapters in Parts I and II. I would also like to thank Gerard Wijers (IBLP, Hilversum) and Maurice van Werkhooven (APS, Utrecht), who provided such constructive yet fundamental criticism of Part III that the publication of this book hung by a thread for a while! Thanks also to Gertjan Schuiling (independent management consultant) and Marleen Nijhuis (Van Nimwegen and Partners, Amsterdam), who read and commented on Parts III and IV at a later stage. And to Selma van Vemde, who managed to enhance a fairly unevocative text with her wonderful illustrations.

For their help with the English translation I would like to thank:

- My dear friend and colleague Nico Swaan who, being Canadian–Dutch and also a very experienced facilitator, was the right person to supervise the translation and compare it with the Dutch original – after which the fortunate appearance of Trevor Ashwin, with his management experience, was just what this manuscript needed.
- Colleagues Bill Critchley and Kathleen King (Ashridge Consulting) for their critical review of the manuscript and for many suggestions for streamlining it to Ashridge Consulting's rich practice of action learning.
- David Pearce (Ashridge Consulting) for sharing his wealth of experience as an action learning facilitator and for introducing me to some of the UK literature.
- Lorraine Oliver for her patience in looking for quantitative 'outcome research' articles about action learning – in other words for the needle in the proverbial haystack, at which she has been wonderfully successful.

I hope that professionals reading this book, whether leafing through it or exploring and experimenting in a more systematic way, will find it contains

1. Or 'young' in fact, compared with other fields. Learning, or 'organisational learning' – didactics, educational psychology, pedagogy – really became a discipline only in the twentieth century.

sufficient information and further references to enable them to organise learning groups themselves, and to revamp their own learning processes when they consider it necessary. I welcome questions and comments – if only because I can never learn enough myself.

Erik de Haan
London, April 2004,
Erik.DeHaan@Ashridge.org.uk
http://home.hetnet.nl/~e.de.haan

Part I

Peer consultation

Introduction
Professional development
through joint reflection

The practice of peer consultation in the professions is a well-established one: lawyers hold 'moot courts' in order to refine their powers of argument; doctors use peer review meetings in order to improve their professional skills, particularly in relation to more difficult cases. Professional development in the form of peer consultation appears to be of vital importance for 'knowledge-intensive service providers' in particular: for service providers, joint reflection on their own practice and its maintenance is a precondition for describing themselves as 'professional'.

In addition to education and training, therefore, joint reflection on their own actions represents a good method for professionals to improve themselves. Subjecting their approach and assumptions to a critical assessment in a familiar setting allows them to share insights and experiences. In addition, they can experiment with new or unorthodox methods without customers or other parties being inconvenienced by the risks inevitably associated with such experimentation or pilot projects. Organised, joint reflection by professionals on their own actions is known as 'peer consultation'. In this Part I I provide an introduction to peer consultation and offer some methodologies. Part IV of this action guide also discusses other forms of joint learning for professionals which are even more blended with the professionals' work projects.

In peer consultation, colleagues discuss problems arising in their own practice in a methodical manner. Participants learn to consult each other about their own work issues, and to handle them in a non-judgemental but instructive way. Someone with an issue or question consults his or her colleagues and learns from them. At the same time, his or her colleagues can develop their consultation skills by working together on the issue. In the process, the participants improve their professional awareness and generate a wider range of views on possible courses of action in a given situation.

1
Peer supervision and action learning: similarities and differences

Two main forms of peer consultation can be distinguished:
- peer supervision, and
- action learning.

This chapter sets out the similarities and differences between these forms of consultation.

Peer supervision: the profession at the centre

The aim of peer supervision is to promote and monitor professional methodology by comparing current procedures with standards and guidelines applied by other professionals from the same discipline. Professionals use peer supervision to discuss specialist knowledge, professional procedures and the organisation of processes. The supervision process comprises the following steps:
1. Deciding on the frequency, participants, agenda and venue of the session and drawing up the supervision criteria.
2. Holding the supervision session and recording conclusions and agreed actions.
3. Implementing agreed actions, such as drawing up and/or adapting guidelines.
4. Evaluating the peer supervision process.

During a peer supervision session, colleagues can exchange their experiences of the use of procedures and arrangements with regard to:
- the structure of projects in interaction with customers, and the recording of meeting outcomes
- implementation and management of projects or assignments
- reporting and evaluation of projects or assignments
- literature and new developments within their own professional spheres.

The main feature of peer supervision is that colleagues investigate whether procedures or arrangements need to be adjusted or redefined. In peer supervision, professionals strive to develop communality with respect to the way in which they work – the professional standard.

A second feature is that a person opens his or her actions up to scrutiny. In so doing, they become a subject of discussion. Based on that discussion and the rules of conduct and guidelines that arise in that context, the professional, with the assistance of colleagues, can explore the extent to which his or her actions are in agreement with guidelines and procedures, and where any adjustments are needed.

Action learning: the professional at the centre

The aim of action learning is to increase a professional's problem solving capacity by evaluating his or her reactions to certain experiences and issues. It focuses on such aspects as how he or she works with others, acts in consultation situations, handles difficult situations with customers and forms opinions. These topics are linked less to the practice of the profession itself, and more to the person in question – the knowledge and skills at his or her disposal, the way in which (s)he acts and makes judgements. This makes action learning suitable for mixed groups of professionals from different disciplines or sub-disciplines.

The process comprises the following stages (for two short manuals on getting action learning started, see Pearce, 1983, and Pedler, 1996):
1. Deciding on the topics.
2. Deciding on the time, participants, agenda and venue of the session.
3. Holding the action learning session.
4. Evaluating the action learning process.

During an action learning session, colleagues can exchange their experiences and questions concerning:
- leading others
- drafting and evaluating proposals
- maintaining relationships with customers and clients
- rejected proposals
- internal evaluation of services rendered to the customer
- external evaluation: measuring outcomes and assessing customer satisfaction
- advising customers and clients
- handling difficult situations, such as differences of opinion with customers and clients
- working together with other professionals.

The main feature of action learning is therefore that a professional has an opportunity to reflect on his or her own actions and thoughts with assistance from colleagues.

A characteristic feature of action learning is that practical issues from the relevant professionals are always the starting point. Sessions are not therapy groups where people delve deeply into their own or other people's personalities. It is useful, however, to consider the way in which the person contributing an issue deals with that issue personally and the extent to which aspects of his or her behaviour may be causing or prolonging it. The discussion can therefore centre on personal performance, but always in the context of practice.

Sessions therefore cover a certain area:

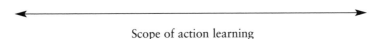

Scope of action learning

1. Issues where content and specialist knowledge are at the centre, and where the latter are to be applied in specific, difficult situations.	2. Issues with a content-related component, but where the way in which the issue holder acts and handles the content is important.	3. Issues where the personal characteristics of the issue holder are at the centre.

1. Issues where content is at the centre will often relate to unexpected experiences, for example in the drafting of memos and proposals. These are often 'what' questions. 'What would you – colleagues – do in such a situation?'
2. Issues where the actions of the person raising the issue – and the way in which (s)he handles the problem – are central are often 'how' questions. 'Can you – colleagues – help me decide how to do or approach this?'
3. Issues where the individual raising the problem is personally at its centre are often 'what' questions again. 'What kind of assignments suit me?' 'What is it about me that makes me come up against this time and again?' Because these are more personal 'what' questions, they can also be asked as 'who' questions, along the lines of 'who is this issue holder as a person?'

Because there is a personal component, it is important for a professional to become aware of his or her actions and to consider alternatives open to them. His colleagues will help him in this respect, primarily by clarifying the issue. They have a consultative role, and aim to help the person asking the question make progress with his or her question or issue.

Peer supervision and action learning: the main differences

If we read the above accounts of supervision and action learning processes, they do not appear to differ that widely. Supervision appears to be

Figure 1.1 *'How does it go again, open-heart surgery?'*

concerned mainly with the discipline, with the profession; action learning appears to broaden the spectrum from there to more personal issues, although still relating to professional practice.

In practice, however, there is a striking difference between supervision and action learning, and this plays such an important role that it is usually not advisable to combine the two in the same session. This difference reflects the evaluative nature of supervision, which can be very disruptive in action learning.

During peer supervision:
- participants decide on contexts, procedures and methods together, and
- investigate whether these arrangements are satisfactory, but

- they also consider together whether they themselves are acting sufficiently in accordance with those arrangements, and
- they talk to each other about it.

During action learning, on the other hand:
- Participants considering a question offered to the group see it much more from the issue holder's perspective.
- Participants support the issue holder in handling or tackling the issue raised.
- They suggest alternatives and relate something of their own experience.
- Usually they do not talk to each other about their behaviour outside the action learning session – the only supervisory, evaluative aspect concerns the participation of action learning group members in the sessions, and the contributions they make themselves.

Peer supervision and action learning clearly differ widely in this respect, and problems can arise either if the issue holder is judged severely in an action learning group or if the issue holder receives obvious, gratuitous support in a supervision group!

Summary: what are peer supervision and action learning?

1. Peer supervision: the profession at the centre

Topics
- Content-related professionalism and knowledge
- Guidelines and procedures
- Models, methods, techniques

Developing communality
Promoting a recognisable style by means of a professional dialogue

Target group
Professionals from a single discipline

2. Action learning: the person at the centre

Topics

1. Issues where content and specialist knowledge are at the centre, and where the latter are to be applied in specific, difficult situations.	2. Issues with a content-related component, but where the way in which the issue holder acts and handles the content is important.	3. Issues where the personal characteristics of the issue holder are at the centre.

Scope of action learning

Target group
Professionals from a single discipline, but also – and preferably – multi-disciplinary groups.

3. The difference

	Supervision	Action learning
Issues	• Profession and discipline-specific issues • Guidelines and procedures • Models, methods, techniques	• Assignment and project-specific issues • Way in which issue holder acts • Personal aspects
Colleagues	One discipline	Multi-disciplinary
Approach	Supervisory, evaluative	Developing, supportive

2
Who or what is at stake?

In peer consultation, a professional with a work-related issue can be helped to decide on a course of action in relation to the issue raised. As issues contributed to a consultation group can range from problems, questions, and specific difficult situations to more general topics, 'issue' is used here as an umbrella term. The professional contributing an issue is referred to as the issue holder – the professional who will hold the issue for that session. The issue holder can be viewed as a client with respect to the rest of the group, including consultants and a facilitator.

The other participants will act as consultants with respect to the issue holder. An important concept for consulting is 'level of intervention'. This has already been discussed in the previous chapter, in relation to the question of the issues which may arise during action learning: content-related technical issues, issues in which the person of the issue holder also plays a role, and issues in which the personality of the issue holder is at the centre. The term 'level of intervention' also relates to this:

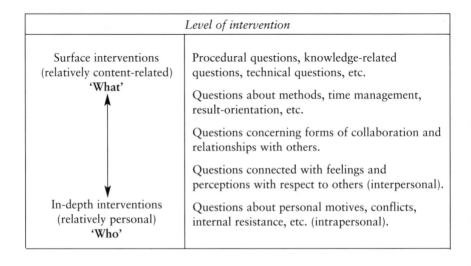

Level of intervention	
Surface interventions (relatively content-related) 'What' ↑	Procedural questions, knowledge-related questions, technical questions, etc.
	Questions about methods, time management, result-orientation, etc.
	Questions concerning forms of collaboration and relationships with others.
	Questions connected with feelings and perceptions with respect to others (interpersonal).
↓ In-depth interventions (relatively personal) 'Who'	Questions about personal motives, conflicts, internal resistance, etc. (intrapersonal).

Questions, issues or problems can thus be rated on a scale. At one end of the scale are 'what' issues, and at the other end of the scale 'who' issues. The 'what' issues are known as 'surface issues', which are not the same thing as superficial issues.

- 'What' issues can be thought of as typical mechanics' problems – they can be handed over to someone else who will deal with them for you.
- 'Who' issues can be thought of as typical counsellors' problems. These are problems which you have to be involved in solving, because you are part of them.

As questions approach the 'who' end of the scale, the 'level of intervention' increases. The scale is illustrated further below, with examples of questions, issues or problems.

Content-related issues about knowledge and its application
For example:
- Where can I find information about absenteeism?
- Who can explain to me how that new instrument works?

Issues about a working method and the way in which problems are tackled
For example:
- I can't get the hang of that new working method – what should I do?
- I have worked this way a couple of times now, but the results are only so-so. What do you think?

Issues about forms of collaboration and working relations with others
For example:
- I am at a loss about the way this project group is functioning.
- I am wondering whether the agreements regarding who does what are effective.

Interpersonal issues: the way in which interactions and relations with others are structured
For example:
- Somehow or other I am not managing to gain that manager's trust.
- How can I get round the fact that my clients keep asking me to provide confidential information?

Intrapersonal issues about motives, standards and values, conflicts, internal resistance, etc.
For example:
- How can I reduce my uncertainty in meetings with potential clients?
- How can I overcome the resistance I feel to contributing issues in action learning sessions?

The question for the consultation group is often deciding what level of intervention is appropriate. At first glance, it seems that peer supervision concentrates more on the surface (content, procedures and working methods) and that deeper levels can also come into play in action learning. But that is not always clear, as the following example illustrates.

An example
A colleague asks what procedure or guidelines (s)he should follow because (s)he is not managing to keep to the number of hours budgeted for a client. This in itself is an issue with substantive aspects, but something else may lie at the root of the problem. Perhaps:
- The colleague is not working efficiently, and so is exceeding the budget.
- The colleague believes that you never say 'no' to a client, even though the client keeps coming up with queries not covered by the plan of action.
- There is no regular consultation with the client to allow discussion of the overrunning budget.
- The colleague doesn't know how to have such a discussion with a client.
- The colleague finds it hard to broach the subject because the relationship with the client is not all that it should be.
- The colleague is afraid that (s)he will get the blame.
- The colleague doesn't know what will happen if the subject is discussed with the client and finds it difficult to enter into an uncertain situation.

In this example, therefore, questions can come into play at different levels of intervention.

During peer supervision and action learning, in the initial exploratory phase, the colleagues approached with this question can consider the potential issues at the various levels. But often it is only when they start to tackle the question that it becomes clear at which level they will have to work. The appropriate level of intervention is often clear from the behaviour of the issue holder:
- If (s)he is extremely relaxed, or perhaps even slightly blasé, the discussion may be taking place at too superficial a level. The issues or potential solutions being raised may be ones that the issue holder has already thought through; they may not come as a surprise to him or her, or yield any new insights. (This need not be a bad thing, if the issue concerned is indeed a surface issue and consultation is taking place at that level.) In order to investigate this, questions should be asked at a slightly deeper level.
- On the other hand, if the issue holder is ill at ease, appears tense or gives evasive answers, the group may be working at too deep a level, or a level which the issue holder has not yet personally reached. In this case, it may

be a good idea to suspend the discussion and explore with the issue holder how (s)he feels, before continuing at a level closer to the surface. In a situation where the issue holder is finding the discussion uncomfortably 'close to home', there is only a small chance that (s)he will be able to learn anything from it. The issue holder is the client and – just as in consultancy situations with your own clients and customers – it is the client in peer supervision and action learning who decides how close (s)he will allow the consultants and their interventions to come.

Often, an appropriate level of intervention is the level directly below the one where the particular issue holder is raising the issue (Harrison, 1970). This is often the level at which an 'anchor point' can be found in order to change something on the level above.

Finding the right level is a matter of trial and error. The key lies in close observation of the issue holder by the colleagues and the facilitator, in order to be able to determine the most appropriate level of intervention.

The intention is that the issue holder should make progress with addressing his or her problem. After completing the last step in a given method, it is

Figure 2.1 *Level of intervention: 'This chap's comments are a bit close to home'*

therefore a good idea to ask whether that is in fact the case; whether (s)he can see what the next step or action might be in the situation raised, whether the colleagues' recommendations can be put into practice. If this is not the case, it may make sense not to stop the discussion yet, but to resume it instead. A starting point might be to explore the issue holder's feelings, and to consider what is lacking in his/her colleagues' recommendations.

Summary: who or what is at stake?

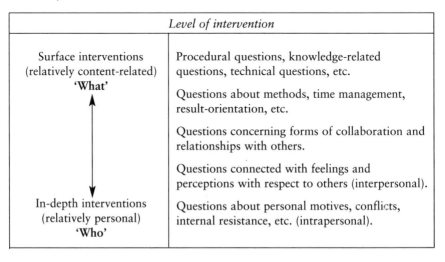

Level of intervention	
Surface interventions (relatively content-related) 'What' ↕ In-depth interventions (relatively personal) 'Who'	Procedural questions, knowledge-related questions, technical questions, etc. Questions about methods, time management, result-orientation, etc. Questions concerning forms of collaboration and relationships with others. Questions connected with feelings and perceptions with respect to others (interpersonal). Questions about personal motives, conflicts, internal resistance, etc. (intrapersonal).

3
The art of asking questions

Asking questions is an important skill when helping others to learn. Broadly speaking, there are two areas on which questions can focus:
- Questions may be asked about a colleague's specific situation in order to reach an independent view or perspective on the position. In this case the questions are directed to the issue itself, and are diagnostic or exploratory in nature. The level of intervention concerned here is the 'surface level'.
- The questions may also be directed towards the issue holders more personally, in order to help them improve their understanding, clarify their options, or confront them with the reality of what they are doing or saying. Deeper levels of intervention come into play here.

An important distinction is that between closed and specific questions on the one hand and open questions on the other.

Closed and specific questions

Closed questions prompt a 'yes' or 'no' answer. For example:
- Do any older people work in that department?
- Have they had a budget surplus before?
- Have you brought up the matter of the return on investment before?

Closed questions often yield factual information about topics raised by the issue holder. A conversation with a lot of closed questions very quickly takes on overtones of an oral examination or even an interrogation, with the person replying being the provider of information – or even a perceived culprit. Benefit accrues principally to the person asking the closed questions, because the answers serve mainly to increase his or her understanding. The issue holder may benefit much less.

Specific questions are also closed in nature, in the sense that only one answer is possible. For example:

- What does long-term absenteeism represent as a percentage of total absenteeism?
- How large is the surplus compared with the total budget?
- When is the return on investment at its highest?

Specific questions often start with interrogative words such as 'who', 'what', 'when' and 'how'. A variant on the specific question is the multiple choice question, where the questioner offers the respondent a number of options to choose from. For example:

- What is the main type of absenteeism – short-term or long-term?
- Are their activities working out cheaper than expected, or are they doing less than they had intended?
- Does the participant do it on his or her own authority, or does the group encourage him or her in it?

Open questions

Open questions encourage reflection and are intended to help someone explore their own thoughts, feelings and experiences. They offer the respondent complete freedom as to the way in which (s)he answers. An open question imposes minimal structure and direction on the answer. One result of an open question is that the questioner receives a longer answer, but something may happen to respondents as well as they listen to themselves talking. This may provide an opportunity for the respondents to consider their viewpoints or mental processes. For example:

- Can you tell me something about your relationship with that manager?
- How have previous attempts on your part worked out?
- What goes on in your mind when your client exercises so much authority?

As a general guideline, ask open questions when the issue holder him/herself is not asking any questions or has stopped asking questions. With luck, open questions can help to clarify a problem, expand perceptions and extend options.

More specifically, the open questions posed to the issue holder by colleagues can focus on four areas that follow on naturally from each other (this classification comes from Schein, 1987):

1. Exploration

In the exploration, the questions are as wide open as possible and may be omitted if they are unnecessary. Respecting silences is important, so economical use of questions is recommended. Open questions that trigger a free exploration may relate to:

a.   The issue.
      For example: What are we talking about? Or: What is the situation?
b.   The issue holder personally.

For example: What do you want to focus on? Or: What matters to you?
c. This conversation.
For example: How can I help? Or: What do you expect from this session?

2. Diagnosis
This type of question can be directed at:
a. A reconstruction.
For example: What events led to this situation?
b. A more specific description, by drawing attention to unspecified words or phrases, such as 'they', 'situation', 'funny feeling', 'unhappy', 'sometimes'.
For example: 'What do you mean by ...?'
c. A more precise description, by drawing attention to generalisations such as 'always', 'never', 'clients', 'the group'.
For example: And what is that like with other clients?
d. A more complete description, by drawing attention to what is being omitted in words or phrases.
For example: What happens if you don't do it?
e. A more detailed explanation of possible 'distortions' (statements which do not appear to agree somehow or other).
For example: someone says: 'When she says that, she blocks me.' What is striking here is that 'me' is put forward only in a passive sense. Question: What do you do when she says that?
f. A clarification of vague or superfluous verbs and adverbs.
For example, 'naturally': What is natural about it?
g. A more in-depth exploration, by supplementing a factual account by a more personal description.
For example: What sort of impression did the conversation make on you at the time?
h. An opportunity to make non-verbal signals more explicit (volume of voice, tone, gestures, where someone is looking). Especially if those signals seem more striking than the content of what is being said, you can draw attention to them by, for example, asking what is going on at that moment.
For example: It is noticeable that your voice changes when you talk about that – what are you trying to express?
i. An invitation to develop hypotheses oneself about what might be going on.
For example: What do you yourself see as the possible causes?

3. Alternatives and consequences
This type of question can be directed at:
a. Exploring underlying intentions.
For example: What do you want to achieve?
b. Listing possible ways of achieving or changing something oneself.
For example: What could you do?
c. Exploring possible ways of influencing others.

For example: What can you do to get them interested?
d. Establishing links between concepts and the issue holder's situation.
   For example: If you relate the x–y theory to your own situation, what possibilities can you see?
e. Mapping the consequences of possible alternatives.
   For example: What might be likely consequences?

4. Confrontation
This type of question can be directed at:
a. Exploring how someone sees him/herself in relation to a problem or a learning issue.
   For example: What does this have to do with you?
b. Asking questions, or continuing to ask questions, about what people think about their own feelings and behaviour, to make them aware of the rules and standards that they apply.
   For example: What happens to you then?
c. Clarifying why it is difficult to achieve intentions, to change or to learn.
   For example: Why do you keep doing that if it doesn't get you what you want?
d. Handling evasive answers.
   For example: I notice that you don't really answer this sort of question. Why is that?

Whether closed, specific or open questions are 'good' depends on the situation. In situations involving knowledge or transfer of experience, closed and specific questions will often help in arriving at a diagnosis of the situation. Where the personality of the issue holder – the way in which (s)he works, or his/her views – are part of the problem, open questions are more appropriate. In any case, it is important for a person to learn how (s)he sees him/herself and others, how (s)he thinks, and so on.

To find out if the issue has a more personal component of this kind, it is advisable to ask a number of open questions at the beginning of every session. This will help you to find the most appropriate level of intervention.

Questions to be handled with care

Chain questions or double questions can be placed one after the other in a single sentence. The questioner asks different questions in a single breath. This often creates confusion in the respondent, for by the time (s)he answers one question the other has often been forgotten. In addition, it is usually impossible to predict which question someone will answer (although it is more likely to be the second one, whereas the first one is often more important to the questioner) and this makes things confusing for the questioner in turn. The questioner risks losing control of the conversation! For example:

• Why is that post taking so long to fill, and who is on the selection committee?

Leading or rhetorical questions have a built-in answer. In a sense, the questioner puts an answer into the respondent's mouth. The respondent is prompted to confirm the questioner's opinion. For example:
• Don't you think it funny that (s)he should do that?

If you are not careful, the respondent will agree with you and you won't find out what (s)he actually thinks. A degree of caution is therefore required with questions of this type. However, questions like these can sometimes be used to provoke someone and draw him or her out: to loosen the tongue.

Structuring and summarising

Besides asking questions, it is often very effective to structure or summarise what the learning colleague is saying, using their own words or paraphrasing in your own. This gives you all a break, while it may offer a chance to assess whether the topic has been exhausted or whether there is more to come. In addition, you are showing that you are paying attention to and listening to the issue holder. What you can also do is ask the issue holder to summarise what (s)he has said.

Figure 3.1 *Questions, questions, questions ...*

Summary: the art of asking questions

1. Types of questions

Closed and specific questions
- Closed questions: questions which prompt a 'yes' or 'no' answer and yield factual information about topics raised by the issue holder.
- Specific questions: questions to which only one answer is possible.

Open questions
- Encourage reflection and are intended to help someone explore thoughts, feelings, experiences, etc.

2. Areas which the conversation can address

Exploration
- Issue
- Issue holder
- This conversation

Diagnosis
- Reconstruction
- Making the description specific with respect to unspecified words/ phrases
- Making the description precise with respect to generalisations
- Making descriptions more complete with respect to what is omitted
- Explaining distortions
- Vague/superfluous verbs and adverbs
- Moving to a deeper level
- Non-verbal signals
- Developing a hypothesis

Alternatives and consequences
- What intentions?
- Listing own possibilities
- Ways of influencing others
- Links between concepts and the issue holder's situation
- Consequences of possible alternatives

Confronting
- Exploring the relationship between issue and issue holder
- Making the issue holder aware of standards and values applied
- Clarifying areas of difficulty
- Handling evasive answers

Summary: the art of asking questions (continued)

---

3. Questions to be handled with care

Chain questions
Questions which succeed each other in a single sentence. This often results in confusion in the respondent and loss of impact on the conversation.

Leading questions
Questions with a built-in answer

4. Structuring and summarising
Gives you a break and a chance to assess whether the topic has been exhausted, and shows that you are paying attention and listening to the issue holder.

4
Consultation methods

During peer consultation, it is important to ensure that the conversation progresses in a methodical manner and to allocate the available time effectively. This will avoid digressions, keep the participants involved, and help foster an open, safe environment. This chapter outlines 15 different methods of consultation.

Facilitators of peer consultation groups can use the following list to help them choose between the various methods. For the actual facilitation of the consultation group, see Part II of this action guide, which is entirely devoted to the facilitation of peer supervision and action learning.

Figure 4.1 '*Shall we devote this entire session to choosing the right method?*'

The order in which different methods are introduced progresses generally from methods focusing primarily on the profession to methods focusing primarily on the professional – that is, from 'what' issues to 'who' issues.

Brief introduction to each method

a. The supervision method

This method is especially suitable for peer supervision. A distinctive feature is that participants make an inventory of experiences, knowledge and understanding concerning procedures, techniques and methods as they are required, or wish, to apply them. Then they consider what could be improved and, possibly, arrange to try out certain alternatives.

b. The brainpicking method

A rapid yet thorough method of distributing information within a group, which also offers a starting point for critical reflection. The information may be new to certain participants, or it may be common to all – different approaches to the same case, or the same working method used with different clients, or different best practices with respect to a single topic. Can also be used to test and compare different approaches to the same problem. Suitable as a reflexive tool for groups of professionals who, although working independently of each other, nevertheless have much in common in terms of subject matter or approach. This method can also be used to make information available to all participants within groups of up to 30 professionals.

c. The problem-solving method and the Balint method

This is a reasonably straightforward method, which can be used effectively in dealing with issues of a content-related or cognitive nature – issues where knowledge plays an important role. The method can be used effectively in supervision sessions. A distinctive feature is that the issue holder first addresses the context of the situation which (s)he is describing. The intention here is to help gain a broader understanding of the issue concerned. Once that 'diagnosis' has been made, the helpers or consultants give their recommendations to the issue holder, who then reacts to those recommendations. The nature of this reaction determines how the group proceeds. If (s)he has been helped, the session can be concluded. If not, the explanation as to why not is then the point of departure for the helpers to ask further questions, and perhaps give different recommendations.

A possible extension of this method, involving the personality of the issue holder more in addressing the problem, is also outlined. With this extension, which draws attention to what is happening here and now in the session, this method has become known as the Balint method.

d. The learn-and-explore method

This method is especially suitable for discussing questions of approach and problems connected with a methodology. The main benefit of this method is that it is eminently suited to 'mutual learning' (see also Chapter 8 of this action guide). The issue contributed acts as a springboard for the conversation, but the other participants also become aware of their own assumptions and presuppositions when approaching such a case. Subsequently, all participants can learn from the exchange of suggestions about an approach or method. The method is suitable for both supervision and action learning.

After the issue holder has outlined the situation and his or her problem with it, there is an opportunity to ask questions. Then each participant defines how (s)he sees the problem. The group members consider each definition in terms of underlying perspectives and assumptions. Then the consultation stage begins – each member explains how (s)he has tackled a similar problem. The final step is to investigate which aspects of the discussion are of value to the issue holder. By examining assumptions and presuppositions, this method takes the participants to deeper levels of intervention. If the issue is not suitable for this approach (perhaps because it is purely a knowledge-based issue), this step – Step 4 in the methodology below – can also be omitted.

e. The dominant-ideas method

A consultation method where the emphasis lies primarily on reflecting on the issue raised, and on developing alternatives to the chosen approach. The dominant-ideas method is useful in peer supervision, because existing best practices can be subjected to a critical evaluation. Moreover, participants in this method can develop alternatives to a chosen approach. The method is primarily an exercise in 'thinking slowly' and deepening understanding through reflection.

f. The U-method

Starting from a specific experience in a specific situation, the group examines the underlying assumptions brought to bear by the issue holder in that situation. Then the participants look for new, more effective assumptions, providing a basis for reviewing the situation. This is a useful method for raising, testing and revising views, norms and values – all of them often held partly subconsciously.

g. Learning from success

Participants in peer supervision and action learning often share issues and situations which call for improvement – in other words, ranging from situations that they themselves are not entirely happy with, through to outright 'worries' and 'failures'. It is worthwhile breaking out of this pattern of constantly discussing sub-optimal experiences in an existing consultation group by injecting some 'learning from success'. It often seems far from easy for participants to contribute a true success story and tell it with pride. However, it can be very instructive and enjoyable to reflect together regularly on things which – sometimes unexpectedly – went well. This method can also be used as an interlude in, or a conclusion to, a session that has been dominated by 'negativity'.

h. The ten-step method
This is an excellent action learning method because it explores the relationship between the personality of the issue holder and the issue which (s)he is raising. A key feature of this method is that it is an exercise in suspending judgment. It is also a method where 'mutual learning' (Chapter 8) comes to the fore because, at different times, the issue holder comments on the relevance of questions and suggestions as (s)he experiences them. Two rounds of questions are followed by a step in which the issue is defined, and often redefined. Mutual consultation is intentionally deferred for as long as possible, and finally replaced by a stage in which participants review the 'actors and factors' that determine why that issue exists in this form.

i. The five-step method
This is an abbreviated version of the ten-step method. It is no longer an exercise in suspending judgment, but a short and useful method for addressing a wide variety of questions. 'Mutual learning' is considered explicitly, and all participants redefine the issue raised.

j. The gossip method
This is also an excellent action learning method, because the participants explore the range of opinions, presuppositions and views that emerge in response to a story told by one member. In that sense, this method is geared to the intra-personal. What is attractive about the method is that it does not require a problem or work 'issue' per se. A 'story' about how someone experiences his or her work and the people involved may also be a valuable starting point. The other participants then 'gossip' about what they heard in the issue holder's story. This method helps the helpers to learn to listen better – 'to read between the lines'.

k. The clinic method
The clinic method differs from the other methods in that it is less geared to discursive analysis and more to active simulation and practice. It works like a golf or tennis clinic, in that participants practise and assess different approaches to the same circumstances. The clinic method is therefore especially suitable for questions that can be translated to a specific conversation situation. The method is used mainly in action learning. In this method, the issue holder demonstrates how (s)he approached a given situation. Colleagues come up with alternatives to that approach, also by

demonstration. Finally, the issue holder chooses a new approach for him/herself and practises that approach in the session itself.

l. The storytelling method

The storytelling method is an action learning method in which the participants' powers of empathy and creativity are encouraged by 'telling stories'. The stories are always true stories. This method was partly inspired by the Raguse method (Raguse and Raguse, 1980).

m. The hologram method

This method is based on the concept of 'the organisation in the mind' (Armstrong, 1997) developed in England. In the same way as a fragment of a hologram still contains the information present in the whole hologram, the issue holder, in his or her emotional experience, tends to reflect the whole organisation or working group to which (s)he belongs. The hologram method helps to explore this emotional trace, and therefore works best with organisational issues where the issue holder forms a part of the context being described, preferably intensively – that is, on a day-to-day basis. Step 3 is similar to the gossip step in the gossip method.

n. Organisation constellations

This method was inspired by the work on 'family constellations' by Bert Hellinger (see Grochowiak and Castella, 2002). The organisation constellaltions method works only for issues with a complex content: that is, for systemic organisational issues where the issue holder actually forms a part of the system described. It is a fairly unorthodox method, and it is sometimes surprising to see how the issue holder learns and what (s)he learns from. From various appointed 'stand-ins' or substitutes, the issue holder collects a substantial number of reflections on his situation. As with the brainpicking method, it is helpful if the group is relatively large.

In the following pages, each method is explained step by step. It is often a good idea for participants to keep the steps of the method they are using close to hand during the session. The time indication given is sometimes a slight underestimate of what is actually required in practice, especially with larger consultation groups.

a. The supervision method

Step	Description	Time
Step 1	*Introduction* This can be done in different ways: • The process facilitator or a participant can introduce a procedure, guideline or agreed working method as a topic of conversation. • A participant can introduce a practical issue in order to test a procedure, guideline or agreed working method. There is also a brief opportunity to 'blow off steam'.	10 min.
Step 2	*Exploration* Professional practice is investigated through asking questions (this can be the practice of one participant, or of several who are then questioned in turn). Round off with conclusions.	20 min.
Step 3	*Reflection* Participants contribute their ideas, experiences and knowledge about 'acting professionally' (in connection with guidelines, procedures or agreed working methods). Round off with conclusions.	20 min.
Step 4	*Appreciative inquiry* Participants compare practical information with the material gathered in the previous step. Boundaries are explored and the group studies the conditions under which it is or is not a problem. Round off with conclusions.	15 min.
Step 5	*Arrangements* Investigate what the results of the previous step mean: what do we tell the responsible manager, what has to change about the way that one or more participants work?	10 min.
Step 6	*Evaluation* How did the conversation go?	10 min.
	Time required	85 min.

b. The brainpicking method

Step	Description	Time
Step 1	*Introduction of the issue* There are at least two issue holders with an issue or case. The issues or cases are interrelated or have a common theme. The group forms into smaller groups around the issue holders.	5 min.
Step 2	*Exploration of the issue* Each subgroup identifies the following for its own case: • Which aspects are important? • What context and wider environment are relevant? • What has already been done – what worked and what did not? • Which concepts and recipes have been applied? • What would the issue holders do differently if they could do it over again?	20 min.
Step 3	*Subgroups share information* From the original subgroups, participants redistribute themselves into the same number of (maximally different) subgroups. The participants tell each other briefly the results of Step 2. They examine the emerging parallels between or additional information concerning the cases.	20 min.
Step 4	*Back to the original subgroups* These subgroups share the additional information learned in Step 3.They attempt to reach conclusions on the issues or cases.	20 min.
Step 5	*Reporting back to the whole group* The issue holders from each subgroup say briefly what they have learned about their case.What does this say about the common theme or the background to the cases or issues raised?	15 min.
Step 6	*Evaluation* The issue holders evaluate the process: experiences, effects of contributions of sub(group) members, etc.	10 min.
	Time required	90 min.

c. The problem-solving method and the Balint method

Step	Description	Time
Step 1	*Introduction of the issue* The issue holder introduces his/her problem and explains it briefly.	5 min.
Step 2	*Exploration of the issue* Group members explore the case by asking questions. Round off with structuring/summary by the issue holder.	15 min.
Step 3	*Discussing solutions* Each group member formulates at least one suggestion or recommendation for the issue holder.	5 min.
Step 4	*Issue holder's response* The issue holder reacts to the recommendations and suggestions: what appeals and what does not? The facilitator asks if we can we conclude the discussion, or if we have to return to Step 2.	5 min.
Step 5	*Evaluation* The issue holder evaluates the process: experiences, effects of group members' contributions, etc.	10 min.
	Time required	40 min.

Extension for the Balint method

Step 4a	*Behaviour during the session* The consultants formulate their impressions about the relationship between the issue holder and the issue on the basis of the issue holder's behaviour and remarks during the session. Why does (s)he have this problem? What is his or her role in causing or prolonging it? The facilitator monitors the quality of the feedback.	15 min.
	Total time required	55 min.

Background to the Balint method

With the addition of intermediate Step 4a, the problem-solving method becomes the Balint method, named after the Hungarian-British psychiatrist Michael Balint, who was affiliated with the London Tavistock Clinic. In his ground-breaking study *The Doctor, His Patient And The Illness* (1957), Balint describes how he experimented with a method which we would now call peer consultation in GPs' 'discussion groups' or 'case conferences'. Various aspects of the study are still relevant today:

- The focus on the personality and behaviour of the professional as a factor in determining the quality of professional practice.
- The valuing of case-oriented peer consultation over individual guidance or supervision, on the grounds that consultation is closer to professional practice.
- The choices made in the composition of groups: approximately eight professionals with similar practices.
- The role of the facilitator as a facilitating primus inter pares.
- The importance of including sufficient rest, slowing down thought processes and suspending judgment.
- The emphasis on free discussion of recent experiences, so free indeed that there were actually only three steps: presentation of the case, discussion and conclusion.

Arguments in favour of the intermediate step which examines the session in the here and now – looking at the relationships within the consultation group as a reflection of the relationship between professional and client – can be found in Gosling et al. (1967), a collection of research results which follow on from Balint's work.

d. The learn-and-explore method

Step	Description	Time
Step 1	*Introduction* The issue holder presents a project and a problem or intended change underlying this project. He or she also illustrates the emergence of these problems/ changes in the course of the project.	10 min.
Step 2	*Exploration* The colleagues ask questions about: • The problem or intended change underlying the project. • Issues or problems with which the issue holder is now confronted (or which (s)he has created). • What new problems (not envisaged at the start of the project) are now arising.	15 min.
Step 3	*Definitions of the problem* Each colleague works out what, in his or her view, is now the dominant issue in the project. All of these problem definitions are noted on a flip-chart sheet.	5 min.
Step 4	*Underlying perspectives* The group runs through the problem definitions one by one to determine what assumptions, evidence or perspectives underlie the problem definition in question. What is it about you that makes you arrive at this definition? What causal relationship is there? Appendix A can be used in this step.	15 min.
Step 5	*Comparative experiences* Each colleague recounts a similar professional experience and the approach that (s)he adopted at the time. This is only done in connection with his or her own definition of the problem. The essential points of the different approaches are again noted on a flip-chart sheet.	15 min.
Step 6	*Connections* The colleagues attempt to explore with the issue holder which aspects of their experiences (Step 5) might come in useful in his or her approach to the project.	10 min.
Step 7	*Evaluation* Review of the process, review of learning experiences.	10 min.
	Time required	80 min.

e. The dominant-ideas method

Step	Description	Time
Step 1	*Introduction of the issue* The issue holder introduces his/her problem and explains it briefly.	5 min.
Step 2	*Identifying dominant ideas* By asking questions and listening intensively, group members attempt to identify which dominant ideas (views, ideals, standards, values, etc.) play a role in the formation of the issue holder's ideas. Possible questions include: • What are the basic assumptions behind the story? • How does the issue holder define his/her own role in the situation and that of others? • What images or metaphors does the issue holder use? (Pay particular attention to his/her choice of words.) • To what extent does the issue holder use implicit idealisations? • What does the issue holder judge as 'good' and what as 'bad'? • Is the description based on facts or interpretations? • To what extent do preconceptions or stereotypes play a role? • Does the issue holder speak in terms of guilt or innocence? • Does the issue holder highlight only negative aspects, or positive ones as well? • Does the issue holder look at similarities or differences? • Are situations seen as static or dynamic?	20 min.
Step 3	*Drawing up a list of dominant ideas* The group members draw up a list of the dominant ideas identified and summarise them on a flip-chart. The issue holder listens attentively but does not react.	10 min.
Step 4	*Issue holder's reactions* The issue holder reacts to the list of dominant ideas and says which of them (s)he recognises as playing a role in the problem. These dominant ideas are circled on the flip-chart.	10 min.
Step 5	*Considering alternative ideas* Helped by the group members, the issue holder now attempts to find alternatives to each of the recognised dominant ideas. These alternative ideas are also written on the flip-chart. The issue holder then explores, still with help from the group members, the extent to which using these alternative ideas sheds a different light on the problem.	20 min.
Step 6	*Evaluation* Issue holder and group members evaluate the consultation process, in terms of both content and procedure	10 min
	Time required	75 min.

f. The U-method

Step	Description	Time	Step	Description	Time
Step 1	*Description* The issue holder describes a situation in connection with the issue and outlines incidents, anecdotes, examples.	10 min.	Step 7	*Evaluation* What has the issue holder gained? How did each member tackle his/her own role?	10 min.
Step 2	*Exploration* Group members explore (by asking questions) and consider with the issue holder, what is characteristic of the description, what is striking about it?	15 min.	Step 6	*Re-description* How might the (original) situation appear on the basis of new assumptions and new behaviour? The group constructs a possible scenario for the new situation.	10 min.
Step 3	*Underlying assumptions* The group attempts to investigate the possible underlying assumptions of the leading figures in the situation. This list is written on the flip-chart.	15 min.	Step 5	*Corresponding behaviour* The group explores which characteristic behaviour or corresponding actions fit in with the new assumptions.	10 min.
Step 4				*Tenable assumptions* The group investigates whether these assumptions are 'tenable', or whether a different new assumption is more 'appropriate'. If they find a new assumption, they write it on the flip-chart.	10 min.
				Time required	80 min.

g. Learning from success

Step	Description	Time
Step 1	*Introduction of successful experiences* The issue holder describes his/her successful experiences, preferably in detail – not only the success itself but also the context. The other participants listen and write down what factors, in their view, made the success possible.	15 min.
Step 2	*Drawing up a list of success factors and context features* Success factors are listed on a flip-chart sheet, possibly divided into initiatives and actions on the part of the issue holder (on the left) and context features (on the right). The issue holder considers, corrects and adds to the list.	15 min.
Step 3	*Deeper exploration* A round of asking questions and listening carefully. From the additional information supplied by the issue holder, and a combination of the success factors, all group members attempt to distil 'discoveries' – previously unnoticed success factors. The new (more fundamental?) success factors are listed on a second sheet.	15 min.
Step 4	*Evaluation* Answer jointly the question: 'What do we learn from this?'	10 min.
	Time required	55 min.

h. The ten-step method

Step	Description	Time
Step 1	*Introduction of the issue* The issue holder introduces his/her problem and explains it briefly.	5 min.
Step 2	*Formulating and drawing up a list of questions* • Each group member formulates up to three questions. • All questions are collected on a flip-chart sheet.	15 min.
Step 3	*Rating the questions* • The issue holder rates each question as warm (W), neutral (N) or cold (C), depending on the degree to which the question approaches the essence of the problem. • The ratings are added to the questions on the flip-chart.	5 min.
Step 4	*Answering the questions* The issue holder gives a concise answer to all questions posed and noted down, independent of their associated ratings.	15 min.
Step 5	*Formulating and answering additional questions* Group members may ask additional questions which are answered immediately by the issue holder. These questions need not be noted on the flip-chart.	15 min.
Step 6	*Definition of problem by group members* Each group member independently formulates the issue holder's problem for him/herself: 'My problem is …' All problem definitions are collected on the flip-chart.	10 min.
Step 7	*Rating the problem definitions* The issue holder rates each problem definition as warm (W), neutral (N) or cold (C).	5 min.
Step 8	*Problem definition by issue holder* The issue holder now formulates his/her problem, as concisely as possible: 'My problem is …' (add to flip-over).	5 min.
Step 9	*Underlying factors* Group members discuss which factors (including those personal to the issue holder) are causing the problem to continue.	15 min.
Step 10	*Evaluation* Issue holder and group members look back at the consultation: • what did the issue holder gain from it? • how did the group members tackle their role?	10 min.
	Time required	100 min.

Suggestions regarding the ten-step method

- In Step 2, all questions are collected on a flip-chart. Because they are set out clearly, this is a good opportunity to take a close look at them. What types of question are they? Are they leading or open? Which level of intervention do they address?
- In Step 6 the participants formulate a definition of the problem as if they were the issue holder. This is the point where the participants can give a different definition than the one put forward by the issue holder in Step 1.
- The issue holder 'decides' him/herself which problem to work on further (Step 8). This may be the original problem, but it often turns out that the issue holder sees his or her own problem rather differently by this stage. Sometimes, in fact, the consultation process can be concluded after this step because the re-definition of the problem has enabled the issue holder to see how to proceed.
- In Step 9 (underlying factors), the gossip step (Step 3) from the gossip method or the Balint step (Step 4a) from the Balint method can be used if desired.
- It is helpful if the issue holder takes notes for him/herself throughout the process.

i. The five-step method

Step	Description	Time
Step 1	*Introduction of the issue* The issue holder introduces his/her problem and explains it briefly.	5 min.
Step 2	*Exploration of the issue* Group members explore the issue by asking questions. In particular, they use an appropriate conversational style (open questions, summaries, listening reactions, silences).	15 min.
Step 3	*Definition of the problem* • Each group member independently formulates one or more problem definitions: 'My problem is ...' • The issue holder, having heard this, re-formulates their issue.	15 min.
Step 4	*Consultation* A second round of questioning where group members help the issue holder to look at ways of dealing with the issue, asking e.g.: • What are your options? • Which barriers to a resolution can you see? • What would you like to explore further right now? • The group members also try to help by trying to uncover factors that seem to stand in the way of solution. They refrain from giving direct advice.	15 min.
Step 5	*Evaluation* The issue holder evaluates the consultation process: experiences, effects of group members' contributions, etc.	10 min.
	Time required	60 min.

j. The gossip method

Step	Description	Time
Step 1	*Introduction of the issue or account of experience* The issue holder introduces his/her problem and explains it briefly or gives an account of an experience (a project in which (s)he is active, observations about the relationship with a customer, etc.).	5 min.
Step 2	*Exploration* Group members explore the issue or experience by asking questions (preferably open questions) and using deeper levels of intervention as much as possible.	15 min.
Step 3	*Gossiping* • The issue holder takes a seat outside the circle, preferably turned away from the group, and does not take any part in the ensuing conversation. (S)he listens attentively and takes notes about aspects that stand out or touch a chord. • Group members gossip about the issue holder's problem and its possible background, causes and solutions. They use the different levels of intervention and ask themselves how the issue holder sees things. What guides his/her behaviour? What is the issue holder seemingly taking for granted? • Group members ultimately arrive at a number of statements indicating what alternatives and what scope might arise if the issue holder were to use different assumptions or take different things for granted.	15 min.
Step 4	*Issue holder's reactions* The issue holder returns to the group and tells the others about his/her experiences as an observer of the gossip phase. What touched a chord? What aspects stood out? Does (s)he reject or accept the statements arrived at by the other participants?	15 min.
Step 5	*Evaluation* Issue holder and group members look back at the consultation: • What did the issue holder gain from it? • How did the group members tackle their role?	10 min.
	Time required	60 min.

Suggestions regarding the gossip method

- The gossip method is eminently suitable for making someone aware of the rules, convictions and assumptions that govern his or her own actions and perceptions. This makes it a method that can help to broaden someone's mindset. The good thing about this 'gossip' is that the issue holder is present. Although (s)he is not allowed to say anything, (s)he can hear how colleagues discuss their impressions of the problem at different levels of intervention. This method can be concluded by asking the issue holder to formulate or re-formulate their own assumptions, issue or problem. The gossip method is also effective in a situation where the issue holder, in the context of a different method, reacts to all advice offered with 'yes, but ...' or 'no, because ...'. The consultants can then gossip about what the issue holder is doing to keep the problem alive.

- Bear in mind that the gossip step (Step 3) can be very taxing for the issue holder, especially when the consultants get carried away with less favourable feedback. For this reason, it is important to limit this step to the agreed time. Also, it is advisable to allow the issue holder some time to return to the larger group before commencing with Step 4.

- The reason why in Step 3 the issue holder is requested to take a seat outside the circle, turned away from the group, without taking any part in the ensuing conversation is that the method works best when the issue holder influences the consultants as little as possible. Any response during the gossip step, even if it be only a change in facial expression or another non-verbal cue, may have a strong and often impairing impact on the flow of the 'gossip'.

- After Step 4, the issue holder can re-formulate his or her question or put forward additional experiences, perhaps arising from other situations.

- The diagrams in Appendix A, which are used to explore how the issue holder perceives, thinks and values, are a useful aid to the gossip method.

- If no one has an issue to contribute, the process facilitator can ask for a volunteer to tell a story about his or her work. Colleagues are instructed to write down what they notice about it; these observations are then discussed with the aid of the gossip method. What do they notice? Does a theme emerge? Does this happen to the storyteller often?

k. The clinic method

Step	Description	Time
Step 1	*Introduction to the situation* The issue holder briefly explains the situation (s)he wants to rehearse and indicates the main problem areas.	5 min.
Step 2	*Demonstration* By using two or more chairs, the issue holder demonstrates how the anticipated or experienced conversation evolves. In one chair, the issue holder plays him/herself; in the other(s), (s)he demonstrates the interlocutors' reactions. By constantly changing chairs and acting out the various roles as naturally as possible, (s)he gives the other group members a clear picture of the way the conversation evolves.	10 min.
Step 3	*Trying out alternatives* Once the situation and the problem areas are sufficiently clear, the issue holder takes the place of the other interlocutor(s) for the remaining period. He or she enters their shoes and acts out their reactions.The other group members now get the opportunity to play the role of the issue holder and to introduce alternative approaches they see. Various group members are given the opportunity to demonstrate their alternative, creating as wide a variety of approaches as possible.	20 min.
Step 4	*Evaluating alternatives* The issue holder indicates which alternatives do or do not seem appealing.	5 min.
Step 5	*Trying out the chosen alternative* The issue holder tries out the alternative that appeals most to him/her, with another group member playing the counterpart. The counterpart's response may be exaggerated slightly, if that is useful.	10 min.
Step 6	*Evaluation* The issue holder evaluates the exercise. The group members provide feedback on behaviour and reactions observed.	10 min.
	Time required	60 min.

l. The storytelling method

Step	Description	Time
Step 1	*Introduction* The issue holder recounts his/her problem as a story, by way of introduction: 'Once upon a time there was ...' The story has an open ending because it runs up to this session and continues beyond it.	5 min.
Step 2	*Exploration* By asking questions, the participants attempt to identify important aspects of the story, such as: • What is the 'essence' for the issue holder? • What is the main influencing factor? • What would the issue holder him/herself have preferred to have done differently or better? • Who are the other persons in the story and what motivates them?	15 min.
Step 3	*Finding and telling stories* Participants are inspired by the issue holder's story to tell a story or anecdote about themselves. It should be a story about something that actually happened to them. • Group members first formulate a number of keywords in their own story. • At least three stories are told, as briefly as possible. The issue holder takes notes during the stories: what appeals to him/her, what is surprising, etc.	20 min.
Step 4	*Reflection* The issue holder reflects aloud on the previous step and, if required, restates his/her own problem more precisely.	10 min.
Step 5	*The sequel to the story* Each group member formulates at least one sequel to the issue holder's story. This may be a 'good outcome' for the issue holder, or it could also be a 'fantastic' result.	15 min.
Step 6	*Evaluation* Issue holder and group members look back at the consultation: • What did the issue holder gain from it? • How did the group members tackle their role?	10 min.
	Time required	75 min.

m. The hologram method

Step	Description	Time
Step 1	*Drawing* The issue holder makes a drawing of the context of the issue to be raised: this may be an organisational chart or a visual impression as a metaphor for the situation. Artistic talent is not important, nor is it necessary to spend too long thinking about it first. A spontaneous drawing is sufficient.	10 min.
Step 2	*Introduction* The issue holder outlines the situation or issue and shows his/her drawing to the group. The drawing is placed in the centre and remains on view for the rest of the consultation process.	5 min.
Step 3	*Exploration* The group members look at the drawing and say what they notice about it, and what the issue holder has left out or not mentioned yet. They 'interpret' the drawing together, in terms such as near/far, full/empty, cheerful/depressing, positioning of figures and positioning of the issue holder him/herself. The issue holder takes notes during the exploration.	15 min.
Step 4	*Further exploration by the issue holder* The issue holder indicates what particular question (s)he is now looking to answer: • 'In relation to my problem, I am particularly concerned with …' • 'My question to you is …'	5 min.
Step 5	*Interpretation* After a short period of preparation, each group member formulates an answer to one or more of the following questions: • How does the environment want the issue holder to feel or behave? • What does the context or organisation do to the issue holder? • What does the environment apparently expect of the issue holder? The issue holder reacts to the interpretations: what appeals to him/her, and what does not?	15 min.
Step 6	*Evaluation** Issue holder and group members look back at the consultation: • What did the issue holder gain from it? • How did the group members tackle their role?	10 min.
	Time required	60 min.

* It is possible to insert an additional step after Step 5 and before Step 6, in which the issue holder receives suggestions on the basis of Step 4.

n. Organisation constellations

Step	Description	Time
Step 1	*Introduction* The issue holder introduces his/her case and explains it briefly. The issue holder also explains his/her own main interest in the case.	5 min.
Step 2	*Constellation* The issue holder chooses a 'stand-in' for all relevant figures from the case. Group members therefore represent people from the case contributed. Group members can stand in for: • Actual people (client, current colleague, etc.) • Also absent people (ex-colleague, future colleague, etc.) • And even groups of people (the marketing department, management team) or abstract concepts ('future', 'ambition'), provided these are experienced by the issue holder as a single entity. The issue holder literally positions the stand-ins in the room, by leading them by the shoulder to the most 'right' or 'true' spot. Important variables here include distance/proximity, inside/outside the group, and orientation with respect to others.	10 min.
Step 3	*Exploration and evaluation* The facilitator asks each stand-in to say 'how it feels to stand here like this'. They are interviewed by the facilitator as (s)he moves around the room, while the issue holder observes from the sidelines. Group members without a role remain seated, watch and take notes about what they notice during this process.	15 min.
Step 4	*Changing the constellation* In consultation with the issue holder, the facilitator now changes the constellation. Changes may be aimed at improvements, but also simply at 'trying something out'. The facilitator can sound out the stand-ins first to see to what extent they want to change position.	10 min.
Step 5	*Re-evaluation* Each group member explains again 'how it feels to stand here like this'. If desired, the issue holder can make changes again or take the place of his own stand-in at the end of each step. Then Step 5 is repeated.	10 min.
Step 6	*Review* Issue holder and group members look back at the consultation: • What did the issue holder gain from it? • How did the group members tackle their role? If any group members did not have a role, they review the process first.	10 min.
	Time required	60 min.

Summary: consultation methods

Peer consultation can take place using a range of different methods. Using these methods, it is possible in principle to cope with any type of contribution.

Some methods are exploratory and systematic in nature:
a. The supervision method
b. The brainpicking method
c. The problem-solving method and the Balint method
d. The learn-and-explore method.

Some methods place slightly more emphasis on underlying driving forces, assumptions and motives:
e. The dominant-ideas method
f. The U-method
g. Learning from success.

Some methods place slightly more emphasis on different perspectives and re-definitions:
h. The ten-step method
i. The five-step method.

Some methods place slightly more emphasis on personal involvement and feedback:
j. The gossip method
k. The clinic method.

Some methods proceed in a more associative manner:
l. The storytelling method
m. The hologram method
n. Organisation constellations.

5
Choosing the right method

The collection of consultation methods should be regarded as a toolbox from which participants can take a range of different tools to help them work on different issues, problems and cases. One difference compared with ordinary tools is that participants in consultation can, in principle, tackle each issue raised in a variety of different ways. Nevertheless, the methods differ widely in use, and a particular type of issue is often better taken forward using one method than another. In addition, there are advantages to be gained in changing methods frequently (variety, creativity), but there are also advantages in working extensively with the same method (depth, trust).

In choosing between the many different methods I tend, more or less explicitly, to use the following criteria:

Figure 5.1 *The art is to choose the right method for each issue raised*

1. *Consulting* – i.e. the method of consultation participants want to choose: more supervisory and evaluative, or more facilitating and supportive? This is the criterion which distinguishes a peer supervision group from an action learning group.
2. *Exploring* – i.e. the way in which participants are to reflect on the issue. Is it the intention to explore the case in depth with respect to the person of the issue holder, or is it to look also at the context: for example, the organisation of the issue holder or other people involved?
3. *Processing* – i.e. the way in which the issue is introduced into this group. Is the group to concentrate on detached reflection, or will it choose also to look at and learn from what is happening here and now within it? For processing the here-and-now of this group, see also Chapter 11.
4. *Concentrating* – i.e. the focus of treatment of the issue. Does the consultation concern one specific situation, such as one specific, difficult conversation? Or is it concerned with a less concentrated issue, such as a series of situations, a project, or an organisational concern?
5. *Transforming* – i.e. the degree to which participants are to explore the issue via observation, reflection and mirroring, or with the aid of other techniques which transform the issue with the help of analogies or metaphors. A more creative discussion also addresses the participants' other senses and talents. For example, they may be asked to produce a drawing, tell stories, or act out a role in the presentation of the issue contributed to the group.

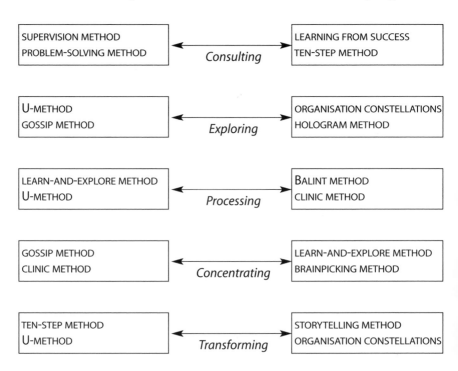

The choice of each criterion should be based partly on the issue raised, and partly on the way in which the consultation group wants to work.

Usually, the choice of method is dominated by one of these five criteria. It is therefore useful to know, with respect to each criterion, which methods lie at the extremes of the scale .

The summary table on the following page sets out each method again, with a score of left, centre or right ('L', '–', 'R') on the five criteria. The methods that score '–' in relation to a given criterion are 'neutral' with respect to that criterion. Methods that often score a '–', such as the Balint method, the U-method, the ten-step method and the five-step method, are the most widely applicable. The table can help to choose between the methods, and also shows where there are similarities between the methods.[1]

1. Not surprisingly, the ten-step method and the five-step method score the same, and the problem-solving method scores virtually the same as the Balint method. there are also numerous similarities between the dominant-ideas method and the U-method, and between organisation constellations and the hologram method.

Summary: choosing the right method

Consultation methods:	Consulting	Exploring	Processing	Concentrating	Transforming
Criteria for choice of method:					
1. Supervision method	L	–	L	–	L
2. Brainpicking method	L	R	L	R	–
3. Problem-solving method	–	R	L	–	L
4. Balint method	–	–	R	–	L
5. Learn-and-explore method	–	–	L	R	L
6. Dominant-ideas method	–	L	–	L	L
7. U–method	–	–	–	L	L
8. Learning from success	R	–	L	–	L
9. Ten-step method	R	–	–	–	L
10. Five-step method	R	–	–	–	L
11. Gossip method	–	L	–	L	L
12. Clinic method	R	L	R	L	R
13. Storytelling method	R	R	L	–	R
14. Hologram method	R	R	–	R	R
15. Organisation constellations	R	R	R	R	R
Keywords as an aide-memoire in using the criteria	L: Supervision	L: Person	L: There and then	L: One situation	L: Reflection
	R: Action learning	R: Context	R: Here and now	R: Project	R: 'Creative'

6

Preconditions: fostering peer supervision and action learning

When it comes to preconditions for peer consultation, it may be useful to remember the acronym 'FOSTER', which summarises six boundary conditions that all seem to be important to address and monitor: Freedom, Openness, Safety, Trust, Expectations and Relevance of issues. I tend to check all six preconditions with group members, not only during the formation of a consultation group, but also regularly and explicitly during its lifetime. I have come to believe that, together, these six preconditions help to 'foster' the learning of the group and its participants.

Freedom

In many service organisations, professionals agree that they will attend at least four (or six, or even ten) peer consultation sessions a year and commit to that as a prerequisite for accreditation. This does not alter the fact that, even in these cases, the professionals attending the sessions do so freely. To a large extent, they decide themselves what to place on the agenda, in what depth to discuss issues and what conclusions to draw for themselves. The main priority is that professionals should learn from this, and learning thrives most if they are intrinsically motivated and determine for themselves the consequences for their actions. At most, they draw each other's attention to situations in which certain professional standards or rules of conduct are at risk of being disregarded.

For the facilitator, 'freedom' is one of the points to bear in mind by, for example, making sure that participants do not use their position or authority to impose their ideas on others (see also Chapter 12).

Openness

Peer consultation should be an open invitation to reflect, prepare action, and learn. Openness to sharing issues and engaging in the issues raised by colleagues is a minimum requirement for peer consultation. The initial openness to the process should be sustained in the exploration of issues, questioning, and the giving and receiving of suggestions.

Safety

It is important that issue holders should perceive the atmosphere in the peer group as sufficiently safe. By contributing a work issue to the group, a participant makes him/herself vulnerable. Safety is guaranteed if colleagues refrain from prescriptive, denigrating or judgmental comments. The aim, after all, is to help someone!

One point to consider here is the composition of the group. If management participate, this may be perceived as threatening because there is a hierarchical relationship between the participants. Sometimes it is difficult to discuss the subject of safety in the group, precisely because the atmosphere in the group is not safe enough. It may be helpful to do this outside the group. The facilitator can approach the participants individually to ask how they experience the sessions in this respect.

Safety can also be furthered by preparation and after-care. Preparation concerns practical matters such as:
• clear agreements
• invitations
• a (usually informal) agenda, with issues for discussion
• suitable premises: a room that is large enough for the group and where it can work undisturbed
• aids (flip-chart, handouts illustrating the steps of the methods to be used, logbook forms, etc.)
• tea/coffee
• preparation of work issues by group members, from session to session (to ensure balance in the group, it is advisable that each member should 'take a turn' regularly).

It is also a good idea to devote attention to after-care:
• follow-up of practical agreements
• openness to individual participants sharing reflections afterwards
• passing on certain issues to management (only if the whole group decides to do so of course)
• keeping records of when sessions took place
• keeping records of who attended, and who did not
• keeping a personal logbook (see Appendix B).

Trust

During a peer consultation session, people describe work issues they are struggling with. Personal aspects are often involved. It is a good idea to agree that matters raised during a session are in principle not discussed outside it.

The facilitator takes 'trust' to heart by establishing a confidentiality agreement. There are three clearly distinguishable options:

1. A 'fully open' consultation group, where everything discussed in the session can be talked about outside the group. This requires the strongest trust

2. A minimum level of confidentiality, where all participants agree that what has been discussed in the group will not be shared with others outside it. In this agreement, participants can continue their consultation among themselves outside the session: they may agree to approach each other with new issues, questions and ideas in the workplace, when needed.

3. 'Strict confidentiality', meaning that everything discussed in the consultation group stays within that group and, specifically, within the sessions. This implies that participants must wait till the next session if they want to make new suggestions or amendments, or if they want to revisit the process of the last session. In between the sessions, the content of the consultation is not discussed, not even one on one.

The 'minimum confidentiality' agreement has the advantage that peer consultation can be more easily applied to projects, clients and the general workplace, and it is also the most popular. However, there may be circumstances under which it is preferable to choose one of the other options.

Expectations

It is useful, especially at the start of a supervision group, to take a moment to consider people's expectations of the peer consultation process and the

Figure 6.1 *If the preconditions are not fulfilled ...*

role of the facilitator. It is important to be aware of each other's expectations and to be able to manage them. As more experience is gained in a supervision or action learning group, participants can re-assess those expectations. Is the session progressing as expected? Should something be changed? The points agreed on between the participants can also include purely practical matters such as:

- the number and frequency of the sessions
- the length of the sessions
- the location and the room
- taking on different roles, including that of the facilitator
- (acceptable) reasons for not participating
- reporting of absence
- the procedure for rescheduling sessions
- the structure of sessions
- the method chosen.

Relevance of issues

It is a good idea to consider the relevance of issues regularly, especially at the start of a supervision group. Practical issues contributed by participants should be:

- not too complicated (in the sense that it takes a long time to explain the situation) – but not too simple (because there is little point in discussing them)
- reasonably current – there is usually little point in discussing something that happened several years ago
- genuine issues – issue holders should be fully 'involved', and not just raise something for form's sake or because it is their turn
- relevant to their own working practice – the issue should be an existing practical issue, not a hypothetical situation.

In short, it is important that issues considered are truly relevant to the issue holder at this point in his or her career. The facilitator may question the relevance of an issue, or help the issue holder to find a reformulation to make the issue more relevant to present-day practice.

Summary: fostering peer supervision and action learning

1. Freedom
Participants largely determine themselves what should be on the agenda and how deeply they discuss matters. The 'client' decides what to do with the advice received from his colleagues.

2. Openness
Peer consultation should be an open invitation to reflect, prepare action, and learn.

3. Safety
- Refrain from prescriptive, denigrating or judgmental comments.
- Avoid hierarchical relationships within the action learning group.
- Devote attention to preparation and after-care.

4. Trust
Possible confidentiality arrangements:
- Fully open: participants trust each other to share information outside the sessions and outside the group.
- Minimally confidential: participants may continue the consultation outside the sessions.
- Strictly confidential: matters discussed during the session are not discussed outside it.

5. Expectations
Manage expectations concerning both the aims of the consultation and practical matters.

6. Relevance of issues
- not too complicated, not too simple
- current
- not hypothetical
- relevant to the issue holder.

Part II

Facilitation

Figure II.1 *A vase or two faces?*

Introduction
Facilitating peer consultation groups

This is Part II of *Learning with Colleagues*. Whereas Part I dealt with peer consultation groups and was intended primarily for participants, Part II looks at the facilitation of consultation groups in greater depth. Since, in more experienced consultation groups, the participants often assume the role of facilitator themselves, this part can be seen as a natural sequel to Part I. This section on facilitation is therefore intended also for experienced participants in peer supervision and/or action learning.

The quality of peer supervision and action learning generally increases if there is someone who takes this quality to heart. Participants are occupied with the issue under discussion. How the conversation itself is going, whether they are getting anywhere near the heart of the matter, how the available time is being used, whether there is a definite structure – questions like these are often put on one side. The facilitator in particular can make a contribution to these questions. The situation is similar to the 'vase/face' illusion shown on the facing page. While the group as a whole is concerned with the foreground – the attractive vase which is the topic of conversation – the facilitator pays attention to what the foreground leaves out: the two faces. The vase represents the issue, and the faces are those of the group members. Just as when confronted by the illusion, it is not possible to see both the issue and the group process – the foreground and background – at the same time. You can only train yourself to shift your attention regularly.

A facilitator stands back slightly from the conversation. While (s)he can ask occasional questions of the person contributing a practical case or offering advice, this is not where the emphasis lies. The emphasis lies primarily on following the conversation and intervening if necessary. The following chapters examine several features of this 'process facilitation'.

7
The role of the facilitator

Who assumes this role?

Any experienced member of a peer supervision group or action learning group is eligible to act as facilitator. The facilitator of peer consultation operates as a sort of 'super team member', doing the same things as the other group members (asking questions, reframing, broadening the issue by reflection, giving feedback, evaluating and so on) only less often because of an additional responsibility for the course of the session. The facilitator will therefore have to consider his or her behaviour in the session more consciously than the other participants.

Facilitation entails taking in what goes on both within the group and within oneself – in order to make sense of the issue and the session, in order to intervene, and in order to find new data to take in. In this continuous cycle of taking in, sensing and intervening, it is important not to venture too far into interpretation. As well as giving undue importance to the facilitator's point of view this could also disrupt the learning by being inaccurate and biased, as interpretations often are (Casey, Roberts and Salaman, 1992).

Peer consultation groups are usually started up by an external facilitator with experience of the methods and of the facilitation of such sessions. The external facilitator then leads (for example) the first five sessions, and attends a further two sessions as a supervisor of the team members facilitating them. It is important to allocate time for evaluating the role of the facilitator. The participants then take over that role and the peer consultation group can continue to operate productively for many years.

Facilitation of peer supervision

The contribution of the facilitator of peer supervision can be structured chronologically, as follows:

Preparation
The process facilitator organises the session. This entails activities like exploring with a manager what activities or duties of professionals are

eligible for discussion, what criteria should be used to assess those activities, and whether guidelines must be drawn up or adjusted. Participants may also be asked in advance if they want certain topics to be discussed, regarding which the facilitator may contact the responsible manager.

Finally, the facilitator can explore the arrangements made during a previous session in order to determine whether the progress made in implementing those arrangements can be put on the session's agenda.

Facilitation

A number of steps are involved in facilitation. The facilitator structures the session and suggests an appropriate method (Chapter 4), and then helps the participants to conduct the supervision itself. Experience has shown that it is important to approach supervision in a structured manner, in order to prevent digressions and to increase trust and safety. The facilitator can play an important role in this. It is also important to create a safe, open atmosphere. Supervision must not be reduced to making evaluative comments – the emphasis should lie on professional action in relation to guidelines and procedures. Where there are discrepancies between action and guidelines or opinions, it is important to list the reasons why this is the case. On that basis, conclusions can be drawn either about the guidelines or about the actions of professionals.

Figure 7.1 *The facilitator as a super team member*

At the end of the session, the facilitator recapitulates the points discussed and conclusions reached.

Finally, the facilitator checks briefly how the participants experienced the session. This may raise points to be taken into account in the next session.

After-care

If the supervision session calls for it, the facilitator ensures that proposals are made to the responsible manager about new guidelines or adjustments to existing guidelines.

Facilitation of action learning

Facilitation of action learning has been described (Casey, 1976) as:
1. Facilitating giving.
2. Facilitating receiving.
3. Clarifying the various processes and methods of action learning.
4. Helping others take over tasks 1, 2 and 3 as much as possible.

During a single session, these activities may encompass the following, in chronological order:

Preparation

The process facilitator also has a preparatory role in action learning, checking with the participants to determine who wants to contribute a work issue. This can also be done at the end of a session, in preparation for the next one.

Facilitation

In action learning, exploring the issue and helping the person with a problem or concern are central. The facilitator often proposes the method, structures the conversation, reminds the participants of the method being employed if they depart from it, and creates an open atmosphere which enables participants to feel free and safe to talk about their concerns.

Here too, the session is evaluated and, where necessary, agreements are made about the action to be taken.

This facilitating role is examined in greater detail in the next chapters.

After-care

In action learning the facilitator usually summarises the points discussed, if only to be able to check out at the next session how the issue holder got on. The facilitator is expected to evaluate the action learning process periodically with the participants, or sometimes with a responsible manager. He or she must, of course, respect the level of confidentiality agreed on by the participants.

Summary: role of the facilitator

---

1. *Facilitation of peer supervision*

Preparation
- drawing up a list of activities and topics
- exploring which agreements made at a previous session are to be put on the agenda.

Facilitation
- introducing the method
- structuring the conversation
- creating an open and safe atmosphere
- recapitulating topics and conclusions
- evaluating the session.

After-care
- making proposals to the responsible manager.

2. *Facilitation of action learning*

Preparation
- inquiring who wants to contribute a work issue.

Facilitation
- introducing the method
- structuring the conversation
- creating an open and safe atmosphere
- evaluating the session.

After-care
- summarising the points discussed
- periodic evaluation.

8
Methodical interpretation of the facilitator's role

This chapter elaborates what can be expected of the facilitator during the peer consultation session. This is done chronologically, from the start to the end of the session.

Some responsibilities of the facilitator (ensuring optimum learning conditions for all participants, monitoring the quality of feedback, and bringing up group dynamic processes during the session) merit discussion at greater length. This is provided in Chapters 9, 10, 11 and 12.

a. Preparation

- Check the room and other requirements such as refreshments, a flip-chart or whiteboard with pens.
- Go through your notes of the previous session and try to picture again what it was like, and what was achieved.
- In some situations, it is worthwhile checking with participants before the meeting to see what issues they want to raise. It may be advisable to ask specific participants to think of issues for the next session.

b. Getting started and choosing a method

Before the conversation starts, it is useful to check out a number of things with the group first. The intention is to get a number of things clear:

- How the issue holder from the previous session got on: what (s)he did with the reflections and perspectives gained.
- What is to be discussed during this session: the issues or concerns individuals wish to explore, the context in which they are placed, the actors involved and similar aspects.
- The reason why someone wants to introduce a particular issue now, and why (s)he is proposing it to the other participants.
- How the group would like to work. How many issues? In what order? It is often helpful to have the luxury of choosing from amongst several

different issues that could be followed, selecting those with the highest urgency and/or relevance for the other participants.
• Which method can best do justice to which issue.

This exploration will result in agreements between the issue holder and the other participants, who will assume the role of 'consultants' for the rest of the session. Those agreements deal with the structure of the session, the consultation method to be chosen, and planning the use of the time available. Once these agreements are clear to everyone, the group can actually get down to work.

The agreements need not remain the same throughout the session. As they work, the participants may develop insights which mean that the arrangements have to be revised. As they talk they may find, for example, that:
• the original issue discussed in the initial exploration has to be revised, or that
• the working method chosen is not generating enough material, or that
• the person contributing an issue notices that other, perhaps deeper factors, play a role.

Such developments may mean returning to the exploration stage, or embarking on a different method, which is applied until something else crops up. In this sense, the exploration is therefore a continuous process. From time to time, the participants consider how the session is going. This reflection may prompt a revision of the arrangements – or provide confirmation that the group is on the right track.

Figure 8.1 *'Amazing how busy our facilitator is. Couldn't he just take a seat and join us?'*

c. Contributing issues

In virtually every method, the issue holder explains his or her own issue as a first step. It is a good idea for the facilitator to:
- reiterate the problem to make sure it has been properly understood and to check whether the issue holder has anything to add
- write the problem on a flip-chart sheet, to let everyone see what it is about
- pay attention to how the situation is presented, to gain an idea of the issue holder's perceptions and how (s)he is dealing with the situation.

Obviously, the facilitator cannot take in all of these aspects from a brief outline of the situation. However, the observations may also be helpful in the other steps of the supervision or action-learning process, whenever the issue holder is speaking.

d. Asking questions

Looking at the issue holder:
- Observing the issue holder, gauging which level of intervention might be appropriate. (Compare with Chapter 2.)
- Deciding whether to interrupt the conversation if the level of intervention is not appropriate.

Looking at the other participants (called consultants from this point on):
- Paying attention to the quality of the questions:
  - Are they closed or specific?
  - Are they open?
  - Are they leading?
  - Does the question imply any judgement or advice?
  - Is there a chain of questions?
- Encouraging a measured, thoughtful pace, by summarising (or having others summarise now and then) and making sure the questions don't come from all sides and head in various directions at once.
- Making sure that each of the consultants is participating in the process and, if they are not, exploring if there are reasons for this which can be addressed.

As soon as consultants start to repeat questions or focus on trivia, the facilitator can suggest wrapping up the question-and-answer session.

e. Exchanging ideas, views, problem descriptions, and so on

- Let the consultants reflect for a moment.
- In turn the consultants present their ideas, views and problem descriptions.

- If necessary, present a definition of the problem yourself as the facilitator if this will be beneficial – usually this is the case only if it is really different from all the other definitions offered.
- Write down the ideas, views and problem definitions on the flip-chart so that the issue holder can absorb them at his or her own pace.
- Allow the issue holder enough time to let everything sink in.

f. Elaboration

- Allow the consultants time to reflect.
- Ask the consultants to offer their perspectives in turn.
- Add your own perspective, if you think that this could be beneficial.
- Give the issue holder the opportunity to react and a chance to say what does or does not appeal to him/her, and what might or might not work.
- If appropriate, elaborate upon a perspective that seems to appeal to the issue holder.
- If no usable perspectives or recommendations are generated, whatever the consultants do; if the issue holder reacts with 'yes, but' or 'no, because' or 'I've already tried that, but it didn't work', an intermediate step can be inserted. The facilitator can ask the consultants, having heard the issue holder's reactions, to explore the various factors – in the situation or in the personality of the issue holder – that are inhibiting progress in tackling the problem. This can be discussed with the issue holder; once there is a better understanding of these factors, the consultation phase can be resumed (see also the 'Balint step' extension of the problem-solving method).
- The facilitator can pay special attention to the quality of the consultation by keeping a record of the questions asked and views contributed by each consultant (for example, on a sheet of paper with a column for each participant).
- This list can then be used in the evaluation, in the sense that each consultant's contribution is analysed in terms of aspects such as:
  - How are his/her questions formulated (clear, understandable, etc.)?
  - How does (s)he present him/herself (involved, active, etc.)?
  - What opinions about interpersonal relationships emerge from the questions (for example, that it is good to work together with others, or to follow, or to be businesslike)?
  - In what tone are questions asked (serious, self-assured, etc.)?
  - To what does (s)he apparently pay greatest attention (order, irregularity, etc.)?
  - What values emerge from this person's questions?
  - What basic assumptions appear to be held by this person?

g. Evaluation

- The facilitator asks both issue holder and consultants to evaluate the process – considering their experiences, the effects of group members' contributions, and so on.
- The facilitator rounds off the discussion of a given issue, maybe looks ahead with the issue holder at action planning, and moves on to another issue.
- At the end the facilitator can also discuss his/her own role, contribution and experiences.

Timetable

The time needed to complete all of the steps in a particular method cannot be established in advance, of course. The times stated beside the various methods in Part I are merely an indication. Usually, an hour to an hour and a half will be needed to work through an entire method. The intention is, of course, that the time should be distributed evenly between the various steps. The facilitator must intervene if the conversation risks repeating itself, or becoming bogged down in unnecessary detail.

Summary: interpreting the facilitator's role

Some of the contributions made by facilitators during peer consultation:

Exploration and choosing a method
- Decide what is at stake.
- Establish why someone wants to introduce it now.
- Get ideas about the working method or form of the conversation.
- From time to time, reflect on how things are going and, if necessary, revise arrangements.

Contributing issues
- Reiterate the problem.
- Write down the problem on a flip-chart sheet.
- Pay attention to how the situation is outlined.

Asking questions
- Observe the issue holder.
- Observe the consultants (other participants).

Exchanging ideas, views, problem definitions, etc.
- Allow enough time for reflection.
- Write on flip-chart.

Elaboration
- Allow enough time to react.
- If appropriate, a perspective can be elaborated further.
- If appropriate, a record can be kept of the questions asked and perspectives or recommendations given by each individual participant.

Evaluation
- Issue holder and consultants evaluate the process.
- Round off the issue at hand, looking forward at action planning.
- At the end: the facilitator evaluates his/her own role and contribution.

Timetable
- An hour to an hour and a half for each issue holder.
- Even distribution between the steps.
- Intervene in the event of repetition or unnecessary detail.

9
Creating conditions for mutual learning

A participant has a work-related issue and raises it during a supervision session or in an action learning group. The participant describes a number of experiences with projects, customers, colleagues or other parties and identifies a particular pattern (or patterns) in these experiences that (s)he wishes to discuss. Alternatively, (s)he is working on a job and the way it is progressing raises certain questions. Perhaps the participant has been given a new assignment and is wondering how best to tackle it. Perhaps (s)he knows that one of the other participants is good at something and wants to draw upon this competency.

The other participants attempt to help their colleague make progress with the issue. Interestingly, they too can see themselves as 'learning colleagues' – indeed, they can learn how to help someone learn something. They can experiment with consulting behaviours, expand their skills, or seek feedback from the learning colleague on how (s)he experiences their input.

The facilitator focuses on these two aspects of learning. On the one hand, (s)he is concerned with the holder of an issue, and will attempt to ensure that their needs are satisfied and that they see a way forward. On the other hand, the facilitator is also concerned with the quality of the consultation process. Indeed, this is a mutual learning process. The person raising a work issue makes progress with it if things go well; the other participants can learn from the way in which they acted as consultants, and from how the issue holder experienced their input.

This holds true in action learning in particular, since one participant is being advised by others – there is one 'recipient'. Consultation is slightly less to the fore in supervision, since the latter is often geared mainly to collective action and evaluation, forming ideas and reflecting on the steps taken.

Suspending judgement

One factor in the success of peer consultation is that, as a facilitator, you encourage the group to take the time to explore the holder's issue thoroughly. What is actually at stake? Who is concerned? Is the problem a symptom of something else? Is there a question behind the question? What does the issue say about the issue holder as a person? At which level of intervention should this issue be approached?

The process facilitator encourages the deferral of judgement by:

- allowing different levels of intervention to play a role (see Chapter 2)
- offering different perspectives from which the consultants can question the issue holder
- encouraging the asking of follow-up questions, and
- summarising regularly, or asking others to do so – this may prompt the issue holder to consider whether or not 'this [statement] sums it up'.

The facilitator encourages the consultants to keep delaying making judgements and offering advice. The main aim is that the consultants make their own sense of the issue holder's problem – which is different from judging it.

Striving for an open approach

A good way of exploring a problem and deferring judgement is to ask open questions. It is vital to understand the issue and the issue holder from the inside, as it were, and not only through detached questioning and putting forward hypotheses. The process facilitator therefore attempts to reflect on the nature of the questions asked by the consultants. Are these questions serving mainly the consultants' understanding or are they also relevant to the issue holder personally? The facilitator can interrupt the conversation from time to time in order to create space for feedback to the consultants.

Figure 9.1 *Mutual learning: 'Wait a minute. Now it's **her** turn again to learn.'*

Exploring the relationship between issue holder and issue

Action learning often relates to issues which arise partly from the way in which people handle situations and their work (Figure 9.1). It is a way of exploring the relationship between issue and issue holder and improving the issue holder's awareness of that relationship. Often, the art is to keep the conversation centred on the person raising an issue, and so to investigate the relationship between issue holder and issue. Moving away from the issue holder has as automatic consequence that the consultants are intervening on the surface level.

An example
A professional contributes the following problem: 'I am carrying out a project for a client. We have agreed what I am to do and have also agreed a price. Now that I have started work, the client keeps asking additional questions or asking if I could have a chat with so-and-so. This is putting me at risk of exceeding the budget. I would like to discuss it with the client in a businesslike manner but I don't want to come across as narrow-minded. How do I strike the right balance between the two?'

Questions that move away from the person:

- In which client organisation is this taking place?
- What sort of assignment is it?
- How is your financial estimate structured?
- How do you yourself view the usefulness of the extra activities?
- What sum is involved?
- Are there compensation options for the extra time?
- What is the importance of this client to your own organisation?
- ... and so on.

Questions that explore the relationship between issue holder and issue:

- What does 'businesslike' mean for you? And what is a 'narrow-minded' mentality?
- What stage are you at?
- How is your relationship with the client?
- How do you feel about the idea of raising this with the client?
- What are your reservations?
- Why can't you say no to the extra work?
- Has this happened to you before?
- ... and so on.

Reversing the focus of attention

For mutual learning to occur, it is useful to reverse roles from time to time, in order to divert attention away from the participant who has raised an issue and to shift it to the consultants attempting to help him or her with it.

Reversing roles is particularly productive if there is some record of the consultants' interventions to use in discussion. Many facilitators keep a systematic account of what happens during the learning process. Concentrate on matters such as:

- What attitude did the consultants adopt – did they concentrate on the issue holder's learning process or did they put forward views and opinions themselves?
- Was their behaviour and attitude congruent with the substance of the ideas they were putting forward?
- What sorts of questions were asked?
- What suggestions or hypotheses were put forward, implicitly or explicitly?
- Were parallels investigated between what is taking place now and how the issue holder describes the situation with a client?
- Did the issue holder give feedback on how (s)he experienced the consultants?

The following chapters examine some of these aspects in greater depth.

Summary: creating conditions for mutual learning

Mutual learning
- The issue holder receives new perspectives on questions and answers.
- The issue holder can compare his/her own approach with those of colleagues.
- The other participants experiment with consulting skills, expand their skills and receive personal feedback.

The facilitator is concerned with
- the issue holder
- the quality of the consultation process.

Points to bear in mind
- deferring judgment – exploring the issue
- open approach – asking open questions
- exploring the relationship between issue holder and issue – the level of intervention
- reversing roles – shifting attention to the consultants.

10
Giving feedback

In a discussion between peers, the participants will frequently give each other feedback.

The aim of feedback is to help the recipient learn something about him or herself. People can use feedback to say something about how they experience someone else, and explore whether issues raised can be linked to experiences which they have with the issue holder in the learning situation. The facilitator monitors whether the feedback is communicated effectively.

Feedback is also useful if the holder of a work issue wants to say something about how (s)he experiences the consultants' input.

Feedback can be solicited or unsolicited. In the case of solicited feedback, the issue holder formulates his or her issue in such a way as to imply that (s)he wants to know how others perceive it.

For example:

- How come I always end up in this situation?
- How can I get round the fact that my clients keep asking me to provide confidential information?

Unsolicited feedback can also be effective, especially from the facilitator. This can be offered if a consultant believes that the issue holder's behaviour in the situation outlined bears similarities to the way (s)he is behaving in the 'here-and-now' situation. By stating your own feelings in the here-and-now situation and giving the issue holder feedback on his or her actions, you can help them make progress. A precondition for this is that you should ask yourself regularly during the session: 'How do I feel at the moment, and how does that relate to how the issue holder is behaving?'

Feedback is information about the effect someone else's behaviour has upon you. The Johari window is a model for giving and receiving feedback. This quadrant derives its name from its devisors: Joseph Luft and Harry Ingham (Luft, 1969). It can be seen as a 'window' through which you give information to others and receive information in return. There are four quadrants:

Figure 10.1 *The blind spot*

Information:	Known to myself	Unknown to myself
Known to others	a. 'public space'	c. 'blind spot'
Unknown to others	b. 'private person'	d. 'unknown territory'

The Johari window (Luft, 1969)

Quadrant a: public space
Behaviour and feelings that others see in you and of which you are aware. A space in which you can move freely.

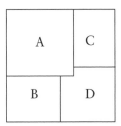

A large free space means that you have an open way of behaving. You give information about yourself easily and are open to feedback from others.

Quadrant b: private person

Behaviour and feelings that you recognise in yourself and of which you are aware, but want to keep hidden from others.

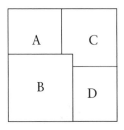

A large private area results if you find it difficult to reveal personal feelings and thoughts.

This may be a drawback in building relationships because you are misunderstood. It may also lead to mistrust or a defensive attitude in others.

Quadrant c: blind spot

Behaviour that others see and recognise, but of which you are unaware.

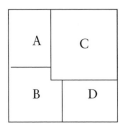

A large blind spot means that your are less self-aware and perhaps don't listen to feedback. This may affect your dealings with others because they react to something of which you yourself are unaware.

Quadrant d: unknown territory

What is happening in the unconscious and is unknown to both yourself and others.

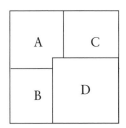

A large unknown area may point to 'hermit' behaviour. It indicates a lack of openness and lack of regard for feedback. As a result, relationships may remain superficial. People with a large unknown area are often hard to predict.

Feedback is geared to increasing the 'free space'.

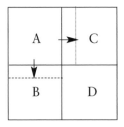

This is done by being open about yourself and listening closely to others. Openness reduces the risk of misunderstanding and projections.

It is not necessary to lay yourself bare and tell everyone everything there is to know about yourself. What is appropriate will change from situation to situation. The idea is to exchange what is important and relevant to a given situation.

Figure 10.3 uses stylised images to demonstrate how someone can transmit messages about someone else. A distinction is drawn between a person's exterior or skin (quadrants A and C in the Johari window: that which we can perceive in the other person, and his/her 'behaviour') and the person's interior or core (quadrants B and D in the Johari window: that which we can only presume in the other person, and his/her 'experiences').

In any circumstance, feedback is only effective if a number of rules are taken into account (see below). Appendix C indicates, in four steps, how to give effective feedback.

Figure 10.2 *Giving feedback*

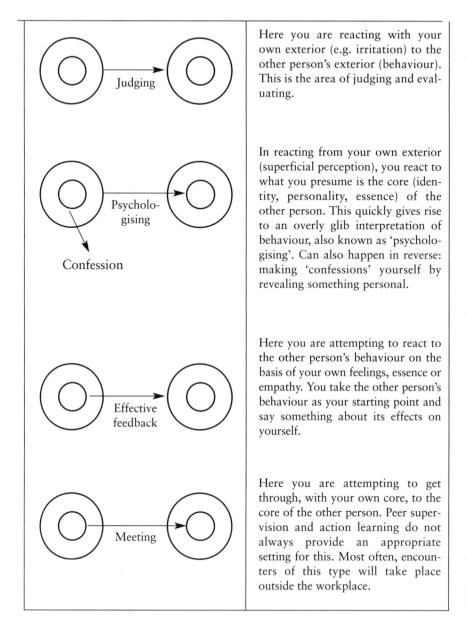

Judging	Here you are reacting with your own exterior (e.g. irritation) to the other person's exterior (behaviour). This is the area of judging and evaluating.
Psycholo-gising — Confession	In reacting from your own exterior (superficial perception), you react to what you presume is the core (identity, personality, essence) of the other person. This quickly gives rise to an overly glib interpretation of behaviour, also known as 'psychologising'. Can also happen in reverse: making 'confessions' yourself by revealing something personal.
Effective feedback	Here you are attempting to react to the other person's behaviour on the basis of your own feelings, essence or empathy. You take the other person's behaviour as your starting point and say something about its effects on yourself.
Meeting	Here you are attempting to get through, with your own core, to the core of the other person. Peer supervision and action learning do not always provide an appropriate setting for this. Most often, encounters of this type will take place outside the workplace.

Figure 10.3 *Modelling feedback*

Do not:	Do:
• Bring up the psyche of the other person.	• Consider the other person's behaviour and its effects on yourself.
• Analyse his/her behaviour.	• Describe his/her behaviour.
• Offer vague hints.	• Be specific.
• Be judgmental.	• Be neutral.
• Give too much at once.	• Give feedback in measured doses.
• Relate only negatives.	• Relate positives as well.
• Allow yourself to be triggered solely by your own need.	• Check out appropriate timing
• Let the other person 'stew'.	• Check how your feedback is received.
• Bring up the past.	• Base it on behaviour in the here-and-now.

Summary: giving feedback

Feedback is:
- Information about your effect on someone else's behaviour – reacting to the other person's behaviour on the basis of your own emphatic ability. You take the other person's behaviour as your starting point and say something about its effects on yourself.
- Focused towards increasing the 'public space'.

The Johari window:
- Public space: behaviour and feelings that others see in you and of which you are aware.
- Private person: behaviour and feelings that you recognise in yourself, and of which you are aware, but want to keep hidden from others.
- Blind spot: behaviour that others see and recognise, but of which you yourself are unaware.
- Unknown territory: what is happening in the unconscious and is unknown both to yourself and others.

Giving feedback:
- From the exterior: based on superficial perception.
- From the core: based on feelings.
- To the exterior: about behaviour.
- To the core: about personality, being.

Tips for giving feedback:
- Consider the other person's behaviour and its effects on yourself.
- Describe his/her behaviour.
- Be specific.
- Neutral.
- In measured doses.
- Positive as well.
- Explore timing.
- Check how it is received.
- Behaviour in the here-and-now.

11
Keeping an eye on the mirror

All in all, what happens during peer supervision and action learning is fairly complicated – when discussing specific situations and experiences, several different 'realities' are always present at the same time. These can be summarised as follows:

	There-and-then	Here-and-now
The topic	1. The issue raised, as it occurred or will occur.	A. What is being discussed now.
Everything but the topic	2. Relevant experiences, standards, values, expectations and wishes of all participants.	B. The interaction between and feelings of all participants during the session.

Something is happening here-and-now that relates to something else there-and-then. Here-and-now refers to there-and-then, but never becomes identical to it. Fascinating phenomena (technically called *transference* phenomena) take place in these exchanges, which can be recognised as reflections of there-and-then in the here-and-now.

As the facilitator of the session, it is important to be aware of the possibility of these phenomena, to recognise them and bring them up for discussion, if only because the participants have to find their way in both worlds (here-and-now and there-and-then). As the facilitator, you can adopt a more detached stance than the participants and so keep better track of both worlds in the discussion. It can be very instructive for participants if you point out any connections you see, and encourage them to watch for possible connections between here-and-now and there-and-then.

The four possible correspondences between here-and-now and there-and-then are discussed in turn below. The here-and-now is seen as a sort of 'illustration' or 'representation' of the there-and-then, which is why the discussion employs metaphors from the field of optics.

a. Through the eyes of the beholder: what are we looking at? (1 ⟶ A)

During peer supervision and action learning, participants discuss an issue or situation *as raised by the issue holder*. Peer consultation works from the following premises:

- All participants are aware of the difference between the situation itself (which is not available to the participants) and the situation as raised by the issue holder – that is, between the following three elements: 'the situation experienced', 'the eyes of the issue holder' and 'the representation of the situation'.
- By raising the issue at this session, the issue holder hopes to become more effective in future situations.

The fact that the issue holder is raising *this* situation and talking about it *in a specific way* says a great deal about what goes on within the issue holder. This person evidently has difficulties with situations of this kind, but also feels drawn to them: now (s)he wants to look back on the situation with the other participants.

Figure 11.1 *Through the eyes of the issue holder*

An example

Someone raises an issue concerning his/her collaboration with another department, which has to evaluate his/her reports on the basis of internally agreed quality standards. As well as appearing arrogant, the department's working method greatly delays the publication of the issue holder's reports. The behaviour of workers in that department is generating pent-up anger.

In their questions, the other members of the action learning group concentrate on that anger, and the fact that it is so bottled up in the situation. Why does the issue holder have so much trouble with self-expression? To what extent does his or her own behaviour reinforce any display of self-importance on the part of that department? The questions focus more and more on inhibitions on the part of the issue holder.

In addition to the situation that has been raised, most methods also pay attention to what the raising of that situation – and the way in which it is raised – says about the issue holder. This is most explicit in the dominant-ideas method. In the clinic method, the issue holder quite literally presents it to the other party (or parties) in the there-and-then situation through his or her own eyes, because (s)he personally acts out the role of the other party or parties in the situation.

In the heat of discussion, participants often forget that there are two sides to any issue raised – the situation or topic, and the point of view. They may spend a long time considering only one of these aspects:

- If participants look only at the issue, the meeting may degenerate into a 'tea-break chat' about factual issues – how badly this or that department operates, that the organisation should do something about it, and so on.
- If participants look only at the issue holder's point of view, the meeting may drift into navel-gazing. All the attention then becomes focused on the issue holder's possible reasons for raising this topic, and the way in which (s)he talks about it. The other figures in the situation and the issue itself are disregarded (see also the example above).

Discussing only one of these two sides of the issue will eventually prove unsatisfactory. It is the facilitator's duty to make sure that both topic and point of view receive adequate attention.

b. The issue becomes the focus of recognition (2 ➤ A)

Through recognition of the issue, or identification, both issue holder and consultants can literally be 'grabbed' by the topic of the meeting. They sometimes get completely wrapped up in it. Indeed, they may well get heated, latch on to the topic and run away with it. The result is a meeting with deeply involved participants immersed in the issue at hand.

An example
In a peer supervision group of managers, the handling of under-perform-
ing employees is a central issue. Each manager has at least one person in
his or her department who (s)he thinks would do better pursuing a career
elsewhere. In most cases, the managers have already had numerous
discussions with the employees concerned, and have drawn up a range of
plans to find more suitable work by mutual agreement. These plans have
led to little change, however. Criticism of the employees' work continues,
and they are not exploring career development opportunities. All of the
managers can identify with the issue so closely that a great deal of steam
is blown off and the group takes little notice of the steps of the agreed
consultation method. They become increasingly vehement – 'What can
you do with people like that?' No one notices that they as managers could
do much more than they have done, and that with better listening they
might achieve more in the session.

The consultants relate strongly to the issue holder's problem – perhaps they
identify easily with him or her, or recognise the irritation expressed. In itself,

Figure 11.2 *Skiing holidays: a focus of recognition*

this 'focus of recognition' is an excellent precondition for a successful consultation session. However, there is a risk that the recognition itself – the sense of involvement or identification – will not be discussed, although it is often interesting to explore as a group what makes this situation so involving for the participants. If a peer supervision or action learning meeting evolves in the manner described here, it helps if the facilitator does not become absorbed in the recognition that (s)he may also experience.

It is advisable for the facilitator to stand even further back than normal in such sessions, allowing space for such an interesting and involved discussion to develop but continuing to observe:

- what remains unaddressed by the participants' recognition
- what implicit standards, values, wishes and assumptions the group is drawing upon.

If the facilitator can add the occasional comment about the involvement and recognition itself, from his or her own more detached position, (s)he can make an important positive contribution from a different viewpoint. However, experience has shown that it is not always easy to raise this involvement as a subject for discussion because the participants sometimes prefer – in their almost irrepressible enthusiasm – to continue with what they are doing. In this case, cool detached reflection may feel unwelcome precisely where it is most needed.

c. Reflections on there-and-then (1 ➤ B)

When a number of professionals are learning together, the meeting sometimes seems to be taking place in a 'hall of mirrors'. Not only what is said in the group, but also the course of the actual interaction between the learning colleagues, is a reflection of what happened in reality, so that the situation in the consultation group implicitly provides insight into the earlier situation. It is as if the 'film' of the past is being replayed, but now with different people in the various roles.

Two variants can be distinguished, as follows.

c1. Parallel reflections: shadow images

In parallel behaviour, the issue holder demonstrates again, here-and-now, his/her behaviour in the situation there-and-then. The situation raised 'casts its shadow before it', in a sense. This phenomenon is common in action learning meetings. In this variant the issue holder makes one or more consultants the 'other party' in the situation. In other words, the issue holder does the same in the here-and-now as (s)he did in the situation under discussion. The consultants in the consultation group start to play out the parallel process with the issue holder, and have an opportunity to become 'shadow consultants' (Schröder, 1974), provided they realise what is happening.

An example
A management consultant introduces a case concerning a long-term reorganisation. As a member of the steering committee responsible for directing the reorganisation, he notices in meetings that his opinions often meet with fierce criticism, although they are drawn from great experience of similar changes. They are not adopted easily – the issue holder has to explain them time and time again and senses gradually that the other steering committee members lack the knowledge and experience necessary for the job.

After the case has been explored in greater depth by the action learning group and illuminated from various angles, and as the questions of the other participants become more specific and more focused, the issue holder begins increasingly to defend his own approach in the reorganisation, adding that the others are now asking about things that are not really at issue in this particular case.

Then one of the consultants notices that this behaviour by the issue holder mirrors the behaviour that he describes in the case. This consultant now brings up the parallel behaviour and asks: 'Does the issue holder think that the other participants in this session are also not up to scratch? Does he think that, like the steering committee members, they lack knowledge and experience? Does he feel misunderstood here too?'

Figure 11.3 *'Did you resolve it like this the last time as well, Mr Pounder?'*

Parallel behaviour often begins unnoticed. As a participant in an action learning session, you often do not realise immediately that you are starting to behave like a protagonist in the situation. Once someone notices it and points it out, however, the discussion cannot continue in the same vein – neither here nor (often) in the situation itself.

Raising the subject of parallel behaviour often results in significant learning benefits. Discussing parallel behaviour leads to a range of behaviour and insights which may also be useful in the case situation 'there and then'.

The facilitator knows that parallel reflections of this type may arise, and can personally observe the situation with the greatest detachment, and so is generally the person best placed to bring this phenomenon to the group's attention.

c2. Inverse reflections: projections

Inverse reflections are precisely the opposite of parallel reflections: in such cases the issue holders no longer unconsciously take on their own roles in the consultation group, but assume the role of their opposite number in the earlier situation.

> *An example*
> Someone introduces a case involving the relationship between herself and a manager whom she is assisting with a complicated absenteeism problem. She is wondering how to motivate this manager better because the latter's energy levels appear to decline frequently, diverting his attention away from the absenteeism problem.
>
> The consultants get down to work on the issue holder's problem, asking questions and developing hypotheses. The situation that emerges appears to resemble the interaction between the issue holder and the manager but is now happening between consultants and issue holder. The issue holder is slightly withdrawn and lacking in energy. She seems to be expecting her consultants to rekindle her enthusiasm.

Here too, there is a representation of the behaviour in the actual situation: in the here-and-now (i.e. in this action learning group) the issue holder assumes the attitude and behaviour of the manager in the situation there-and-then, while the consultants assume the behaviour of the issue holder in the situation under discussion.

This may happen because the consultants recognise the situation and are unconsciously relating it to their own experiences, as in $(2 \longrightarrow A)$.

Overlapping experiences give rise to overlapping feelings of powerlessness. The powerlessness in the here-and-now has shifted from the issue holder – who felt it there-and-then – to the consultants. In the preceding example, everyone keeps passing on their own feelings of powerlessness:

Figure 11.4 *Inverse behaviour: how an earlier experience can be passed on*

1. The manager has been contaminated by the powerlessness within his department in tackling the absenteeism problem: '*What must I do to help my people make progress?*'
2. The issue holder feels powerless in relation to the manager: '*What must I do to get this man enthusiastic about my approach to absenteeism?*'
3. The issue holder shows his powerlessness in the consultation group (here-and-now), so that the consultants also start to feel powerless: '*What must we do to give the issue holder a sense of purpose again?*'
4. It is even possible that the powerlessness may affect the facilitator at a later stage, in other words when the group gets stuck: '*What must I do to get this consultation group moving again?*'

The whole process starts with the assumption that someone else can and must be motivated and that 'I' am the person to do it. The manager first makes this assumption implicitly and unconsciously, then the issue holder, and finally the consultants during the action learning session. An assumption like this often points to a need – for example, in this case the need to avoid or root out feelings of powerlessness. And this need points in turn to another need, or a fantasy, namely that of having everything completely under control, of being omnipotent.

This shows that consultants in consultation groups must be careful about living up to the expectations which the issue holder brings to the session. This might merely reinforce a need for and belief in omnipotence ('This is how you motivate people!'). This might in turn reinforce the issue holder's tendency to 'act powerless' in the session, as was the manager's tendency in the case study.

The consultants can do something else instead. They can help the issue holder see that what (s)he is doing with them now mirrors what the manager did earlier. They can explore the reflection or likeness between the situation now and the issue holder's case of the poorly motivated manager.

In this way, issue holders can see in others and learn from others what they personally experienced previously. This may increase their awareness of the way in which they themselves have defined a situation. The consultants can then treat issue holders in the same way as the issue holders might treat the poorly motivated manager. In the here-and-now, and later in the then-and-there, this process enables the parties concerned to redefine their situation.

The issue holders can discover what to do in the situation, by looking at how the consultants are now treating them, but can also note what feelings that treatment engenders in them as the recipient. The consultants can reflect on the issue holders' expectations, needs or feelings, and explore their possible sources.

As already mentioned, the issue holders can engineer this type of conversation with their managers, inviting them to explore the source of apathetic, poorly motivated attitudes.

For another frequent example of inverse reflections, the passing on of feelings of anger, see Figure 11.4.

d. Lack of focus: diffuse scatter (2 ➡ B)

Sometimes what happens in a consultation group has nothing to do with the issue. However, even these situations are learning opportunities and therefore relevant for facilitators. These are situations with little focus: group members spend time together, sometimes even in an intense and energetic manner, but they do not consult each other and they hardly inquire about the issues raised. The group seems to meet more for entertainment purposes, to keep themselves busy.

The task of a consultation group is to work here-and-now on the issue holder's problem, to learn something about it in a group context. But it need not be the case that the group works on the task here-and-now – it may be that everything but the issue prevails. Often, a consultation group which is not addressing the set task nevertheless gives the impression of working intensively and meaningfully. Such a group, acting as if it were addressing the task, was termed a 'basic assumption group' by Wilfred Bion, the English psychiatrist who was the first to describe groups of this kind (Bion, 1961). These 'groups that act as if' are referred to below as 'as if groups'.

An example
An action learning group which has been meeting for some time has recently been having trouble finding issue holders. The session always starts with the same ritual – the words 'Who has an issue this time?' followed by a frosty silence. Time and time again, but with growing and evident reluctance, the same group member – an ambitious young man – eventually steps forward. When the group starts work on his issue, it is noticeable that he is speaking virtually all of the time and the other members are passive and listless. If they say anything, they make it clear that they do not really relate to the issue and that things are handled differently in their own departments. Only at the end of the session, when it is suggested that the group should stop meeting, is the group galvanised into action – most of the members protest against the suggestion and assure each other that they found the session very useful.

Why would a group do something other than addressing the set task? Is it possible to see advantages in working on the task, but also in *not* working on the task?

Advantages of the 'work group'	Advantages of the 'as if group'
• Enjoyment in working on something; creating something. Ability to look critically at progress and effectiveness. • Daring to face up to reality. • Self-development, learning from the discussion of experiences and behaviour. • Expressing individual wishes and objectives. • Common task and results.	• Enjoyment of being active, but without having to assume responsibility. • Being able to escape reality. • Not having to bother with 'painful' issues. • Becoming wrapped up in common wishes and objectives. • Common objectives and atmosphere.

Three different types of 'as if' group are often distinguished in the literature (Bion, 1961):
• *Dependency groups* act as if the task is to satisfy the wishes and needs of the participants. Group members behave dependently, putting off opinion-forming and decision-making to the next session or until someone with more authority has expressed an opinion.
• *Fight/flight groups* act as if the task is to defend themselves against an external risk or threat. Group members behave irritably, anxiously or in a protesting manner.
• *Pairing groups* act as if the task is to sit and await some wonderful future event that will make everything better. Group members behave hopefully,

expectantly and sometimes even euphorically, without taking any practical steps towards achieving their wonderful future. Often, the hope of something better is embodied in a pair of group members who focus on each other. After the session, individual members are often left with a feeling of disappointment and failure, which quickly gives way to the hope that the next time will be better.

In general, an 'as if' group lacks a number of things that are essential for peer consultation: being interested in reflection, defining the task or problem, paying attention to the use of time, using critical faculties, distinguishing and using individual qualities, and so on. However, 'as if' groups need not be avoided in every situation. Type 1 sometimes has advantages for people in helping professions who have to work in depressing situations; Type 2 has advantages for an army in a state of war; Type 3 may be useful in direct marketing organisations. All such cases involve 'sophisticated use of as if behaviour' (see Obholzer and Zagier Roberts, 1994). However, it is virtually impossible to make sophisticated use of such behaviour in consultation groups. Indeed, in order to get the consultation off the ground, it should be eliminated as fully as possible.

The facilitator plays an important role in 'as if' groups, if only because such groups unconsciously appeal to their leader to preserve the behaviour in which they are engaged: in Type 1 groups, an appeal to fulfil group members' wishes by being pleasant and considerate; in Type 2 groups, to identify a threat and

Figure 11.5 *Lack of focus: the group meets for entertainment*

leading the attack or escape; and in Type 3 groups, to foster hope or the belief that the leader is all-knowing and all-powerful.

This puts the facilitator in a difficult position. If (s)he answers the appeal the 'as if' state of mind will be preserved and little learning will take place, but thwarting it – for example, by openly reflecting on how the session is progressing – runs the risk of losing authority. The facilitator may then discover that (s)he is the only one who views the session in this particular way, and that the other group members argue passionately that they are doing very well.

It is hard to do the right thing as a facilitator of 'as if' groups, so it makes sense to try to maintain a certain distance, and to avoid being dragged along by the prevailing type of behaviour. Careful reflection, asking questions and encouraging members to return to the task at hand perhaps represent the only way to make an 'as if' group a work group again.

Conclusion

Reflections and connections between here-and-now and there-and-then are essential for a successful peer consultation session. These reflections give all participants, especially the issue holder, the opportunity to prepare themselves in the here-and-now for the there-and-then. This increases the likelihood that they will do things during the peer supervision or action learning process that will also have an effect on their behaviour and working methods in real work situations.

The following two activities can help enable reflections and connections that will help members of a consultation group to do their jobs as effectively as possible:
1. Pointing out the occurrence of connections and so making everyone aware of them.
2. Alternating between different types of connections, for example by asking the following questions if they have not been raised very much:
   - Issue holder and point of view. 1 ➤ A: 'What is it that makes the case worthwhile to discuss for you personally?'
   - Focus of recognition. 2 ➤ A: 'What are (the differences between) everyone's own experiences in this area?' (see also Step 5 in the learn-and-explore method).
   - Reflections of there-and-then. 1 ➤ B:
     (*parallel*) 'In your view, are there similarities between this situation here-and-now and the situation which you have raised?'
     (*inverse*) 'Is there something in your behaviour now that resembles the behaviour of the other person you are describing?'
   - Diffuse scattering. 2 ➤ B: 'Is this what we should be talking about here-and-now?'

In both activities, the facilitator of the session can take the lead.

More generally, peer consultation requires everyone concerned to become sensitive to the way in which the learning situation is developing here-and-now, and keep asking themselves whether this learning situation says something about the issue at hand.

Summary: keeping an eye on the mirror

The interaction between consultation group participants as a reflection of reality

1. The situation and point of view of the issue holder
    The issue holder always reveals something of him/herself when raising the situation.

2. A focus of recognition
    The consultants become involved to a greater or lesser extent in the issue holder's situation.

3a. Parallel behaviour
    The issue holder sometimes demonstrates the attitude and behaviour which (s)he also displays in the situation in question, and so invites the consultants to adopt the behaviour of the other person(s) in the situation.

3b. Mirroring behaviour
    The issue holder sometimes assumes the attitude and behaviour of his or her client/manager, and so invites the consultants to adopt the behaviour (s)he exhibits in the situation.

4. Loss of focus
    The group is no longer devoting itself to the set task. Different, partly unconscious, wishes and desires are distracting the members.

It is effective to devote attention explicitly to:

• Making the interaction as it is in the here-and-now explicit by pointing it out.
• Exploring whether something is happening now that also occurs in the situation under discussion.
• Exploring whether other members are unconsciously attempting to fulfil implicit expectations of the issue holder.
• Alternating and switching between different connections between the situation now, the situation then, and a range of other situations and experiences.
• Exploring whether and how the learning situation here-and-now is evolving, and whether anything can be done to improve it.

The facilitator of the session can take the lead in this respect.

12
Encouraging development

The success of peer consultation stands or falls with the quality of the consultation group as a 'learning group'. A group of colleagues who want to help each other become more professional by means of consultation should be not only 'working well' but also 'developing well'. There are a variety of influences outside and inside the group, such as organisational politics or emerging dominant personalities, which may inhibit concentration on work and development. Facilitators of consultation groups should develop their sensitivity to threatening and encouraging aspects of work and development in groups.

Encouraging consultation

Working well means that the group has sufficient attention, focus and nerve to devote itself to the task in hand: discussing difficult issues and situations involved in the participants' own practice. This makes several demands of group members:

- In the role of issue holder they must be prepared to introduce 'real' practical issues (see Chapter 6) and handle them in an enquiring manner, opening themselves up to sometimes painful feedback and advice.
- In the role of consultant they must commit themselves entirely to a colleague's issue and, in exploring that issue, put their colleague – rather than their own curiosity – at the centre of attention. This calls for certain consultation skills on their part, to support the issue holder in working on their own case. It also requires that they be prepared to learn in the field of consultation, by listening closely to feedback from the issue holder and the other group members.
- In the role of process facilitator colleagues must be prepared to 'let go' of the case itself and devote themselves more to the 'background' of the discussion, that is to say, the way in which the group is working on the case.
- Moreover, it is important that all group members should establish close cooperation between process facilitator and participants – in

other words, they should respectively have the courage to take the lead, and support and follow the process facilitator.

Consultation is an activity that requires a great deal of concentration and creativity, for which it is necessary to reserve sufficient time and energy. This can easily be overlooked, especially if the consultation is with colleagues from the same organisation and is held at the place of work. However, a half-hearted approach to consultation will never produce adequate results: group members will experience the consultation as unsatisfactory, a waste of time, useless. Organisations increasingly attempt to fit consultation in around the edges of the working week – for example, from six to eight in the evening so that their 'busy working practice doesn't suffer'. In general, evenings prove to be a bad time for consultation – participants are already slumped bleary-eyed in their chairs and the actual consultation is a long time in taking shape.

It often becomes clear later on that two hours was not sufficient time to achieve the necessary depth. It is therefore recommended that peer consultation takes place only if it can be scheduled within working hours and if all participants are prepared to set aside at least two and a half hours per session. Three hours is enough time to explore a case in depth, including a thorough discussion of the actions of consultants and process facilitator, or to examine two cases sufficiently with time left over to discuss the facilitation.

In my view, 'routine' and 'stress' are the greatest enemies of consultation work. Groups can often be caught between them as if between the proverbial 'rock and hard place'. Routine can develop as a result of working in groups of colleagues who meet frequently in the workplace as well. They will tend to repeat communication patterns that occur there, without making them explicit. If we do the same thing in a consultation group as we do in the workplace, or if we repeat what happened in previous sessions, we create dull conversations that are not conducive to learning anything new.

On the other hand, stress too can permeate the consultation group in a counterproductive way. It is important to exclude the stress and hectic pace of work from the consultation process. A hasty, businesslike, efficient but entirely predictable consultation is in fact more harmful than no consultation at all – the benefit of calm reflection and of waiting for an original, provocative thought to be raised is entirely lost. The session starts to resemble an ordinary meeting, so that the additional stress of the 'lost' hours becomes painfully clear. Properly conducted consultation, on the other hand, can be useful in alleviating stress, provided the group can devote real attention to the issue at hand.

Another way in which stress can build up in a consultation group is when organisational decisions and organisational politics influence the consultation process. For example:

Figure 12.1 *In order to encourage work and development in the consultation group, the facilitator addresses its background: the way the consultation is taking place, what the group members are leaving out in their conversations and what binds them together. (See the 'vase/face' illusion, Figure II.1.)*

- If there are hierarchical relationships within the consultation group, especially at the times of appraisal reviews or when employees want something from their managers.
- In the context of an organisational change such as a reorganisation or merger, which leads employees to disagree on the action to be taken and divide into coalitions.
- If there are double or hidden agendas, internal competition or an organisational culture which is not experienced as particularly safe.

In general terms, novice consultation groups must beware of organisational politics – I would recommend, for example, that managers and their direct supervisees are placed in different groups. However, this in itself may represent an 'easy' solution, which may lead to avoidance of the real problems. The ideal situation is one where if political relationships do exist between members of consultation groups they can be discussed in an open and instructive manner. This also avoids the 'routine' of repeating the often-automatic avoidance and compartmentalisation of issues related to power and politics in teams and organisations. This being said, peer supervision is by nature more evaluative than action learning, in which case it is sometimes essential to have different hierarchical levels represented in the group.

After paying such attention to issues of routine and stress, it may be useful to say that it is very rare for people to get bored in a consultation group or to feel unproductive pressure. If this does happen, members can always say so – in virtually every case, the pattern of interaction will change immediately and it is possible to find a different, more instructive way of working.

Encouraging group development

If a learning group is developing well, it is evolving over time towards:
- more 'sensitive' and 'relevant' cases
- better case discussion (e.g. with higher-quality listening, and better asking and reformulation of questions)
- more and better feedback, leading to increasing learning opportunities for consultants and facilitators
- visible effects on the group members' own working practice
- greater willingness to consider the development of the group itself.

In my experience, the development of a consultation group frequently follows a predictable sequence of stages. These are also described in the literature (Schutz, 1958).

1. At the start, it is often necessary to remove a whole range of barriers – participants are ambivalent about their decision to take part in the group, or experience their decision as inspired partly by external motives. In addition, participants often feel anxiety about having to contribute something personal, or a view about which they still have many doubts themselves.

2. This *inclusion* stage (Schutz, 1958 – 'Do I belong here?'; 'Do I want to take part in this?'; 'Do I have the nerve for this?') is sometimes followed by a *control* stage in which the nature of the learning group itself is discussed. 'What issues should be discussed?' 'Why are we sitting here?' 'Do we all have to participate in the same way, and to the same degree?' 'What do we regard as an appropriate, or an inappropriate, issue?'

3. If a consultation group continues to meet and these stages are overcome, however, eventually the participants will start to appreciate the consultation's value to their own working practice or personal development. They also start to realise how important the other group members have become to their own learning process. A positive dynamic results, with enthusiastic participants and a good turnout (Schutz's *affection* stage). Now the participants are much more aware of the things that they all share. However, a new risk is that attention to differences will be repressed. The session may generate plenty of recognition and communality, but less pronounced or provocative feedback.

4. To overcome the previous stage and give space to critical voices again, it is often necessary to recruit new members or invite an external coach back to the group.
5. If critical ability and diversity within the group can be recovered, this is followed by a new stage which has the characteristics of 'inclusion' again. It may not now be certain that all of the consultation group members want to continue, and each takes stock.

The application of Schutz's group development model to consultation groups is summarised in the table below. It should be noted that longer-established consultation groups will keep revisiting the control and affection phases as well.

Phase	Name	Theme	Area of tension	How to recognise it
1.	Inclusion	'Do I belong here?'	Inside vs. outside	Cancellations Scarcity of contributions A 'wait-and-see' attitude
2.	Control	'Who has the final word?'	On top vs. underneath	High intensity Scoring points off each other 'Clever' feedback which meets with compliments
3.	Affection	'Do I like them?'	Nearby vs. far away	Enthusiasm Pride in being part of the group 'Cautious' feedback
4.	Inclusion	'Do I still belong here?'	Inside vs. outside	Review New readiness to take risks One or two members leave and/or are recruited

It is important to stress that I myself am seldom present throughout this development process, because my aim is to make myself superfluous quickly and invite group members to take on the role of facilitator as soon as possible. If I do stay, my own role shifts to that of consultant within the group and coach to the facilitators. It is noticeable that virtually all group members struggle with the facilitator's role, mainly because it means they have to step outside the peer communication context temporarily and adopt a meta-position with respect to their colleagues. This is usually accompanied by tension. Important questions – 'Will my colleagues allow me such a position?'; 'Can I separate the content from the process?'; 'How "controlling" am I expected to be?'; 'How should I consult or intervene from this role?' – inevitably arise. I myself find the facilitator's role very complex, even without being a close colleague of the group members. I tend to become self-critical and think afterwards that it could have gone much better, that a whole range of relevant observations were left out, or that too much was included. I also notice that members of consultation groups feel they themselves have much to learn before they can act as facilitators. It is worth giving it a try, however. The role of facilitator – like that of consultant – can often be applied in your own work as well, for example when chairing project or management teams.

It is certainly not a luxury to start a new consultation group with a more experienced facilitator. He or she can start to step back after three sessions (say, via the role of group supervisor), and after five to eight sessions let the group carry on by itself, possibly returning once if the group has been lingering for a while in Phase 3 (the 'affection phase'). An external facilitator can often help spur the group on to more open feedback. At the end of each consultation session – not just after the first few sessions! – it is also worth spending at least five minutes reflecting as a group on the quality of the facilitation.

An example
A consultation group of eight senior staff members in a government department is meeting for the fifth time. On this occasion no less than five members are absent, due to holiday, leave, illness, pressure of work, and an unknown reason. The first question to ask is: 'Does this mean something? Does this say something about the way we have been working?' The immediate counter-question from one of the members is: 'Are we actually a group? Are we actually building something here?' As the questioning continues, the focus of this member's annoyance seems to be another member who has not yet contributed any personal issues to the sessions. The member in question reacts defensively: 'I'm learning a lot, especially about listening, and I'm pleased to have acquired the courage to ask questions. For me, that's quite risky in itself.' On closer examination, this group appears to have created a number of 'types' in the course of its existence – the timid person too afraid to contribute a case, the alert one who regularly asks critical questions about others' contributions and the progress of the group, the eager beaver who is prepared to introduce the same case every time using a different wording, the enthusiastic head of Human Resources who conducts spontaneous progress surveys off his own bat and is initiating new other groups all over the organization. Very slowly, and partly thanks to the large number of absentees voting with their feet, it becomes possible to discuss these unique contributions and put the development of the group itself on the agenda.

A high-quality learning group is prepared to consider its own development as a group, to put it explicitly on the agenda and, if necessary, to change it. This also relates to the adoption of certain roles within the

Figure 12.2 *Inclusion, control and affection are what you need for effective group development*

learning group concerning needs such as responsibility, thoughtfulness, conscientiousness, critical thinking and result orientation. Often, these themes keep cropping up in the contributions of individuals who, more or less subconsciously, take it upon themselves to look after that theme. Bion (1961) calls this natural preparedness or susceptibility of an individual to enter into a special relationship with the rest of the group, *valency*. For example, different group members appear to have different valencies at different times relating to inclusion, control and affection. They may find themselves being the only one to include others in conversation, to exercise control or to express affection. When valencies play out in a more extreme manner, this can lead to the emergence of prophets or scapegoats – 'one-dimensional' group members about whose contributions the rest of the group (and often they themselves!) are in full agreement. A role interpretation determined by valency sometimes impedes learning, because learning requires group members to be able to step back from their automatic role preferences and experiment with qualities that are not their natural strengths. With regard to valencies and group development, it is useful to update the 'Process facilitator's logbook' (Appendix B.2) together at the end of each session.

Summary: encouraging development

In order to encourage *work* in the peer consultation group, the facilitator can pay attention to the following aspects:
- The ability of the issue holder to introduce issues of personal relevance.
- The ability of the consultants to put the issue holder at the centre of the conversation.
- The right balance between the *routine* of automatic communication patterns and the *stress* from pressure of work and lack of time.
- Any possible 'political' component in the group, deriving from the work relationships between group members or from coalitions in the workplace.

Over time, facilitators can encourage the consultation group in its development as a learning group:
- From admission or *inclusion*, to agreeing of standards or *control*, to experiencing nearness or *affection*, to reviewing at a higher level (*inclusion*), to creating new standards (*control*), and so on.
- The group members can share the facilitation process to an increasing degree. From time to time the group as a whole may need an external coach, to help it move through certain developmental stages.
- Like organisational politics, individual dispositions or *valencies* can affect group dynamics.

The facilitator of the session can take the lead in the discussion of individual valencies and group development.

13
Handling difficult moments

Meeting with colleagues and having the opportunity to talk about your work, and what you find interesting and annoying about it, can be very enjoyable. It can help you in becoming more professional in your discipline and taking advantage of colleagues' knowledge, as well as letting you assist in the development of others who may have less experience and know-how than yourself. You can also make a contribution to developing arrangements and procedures which lead, for example, to a better service to clients.

However, we all know from our own experience that development and learning also entail feelings of uncertainty and tension (see also Chapter 18). This always comes into play to some degree in supervision and action learning:

- People are discussing sensitive matters that relate to themselves – not just things that are going well, but also their weaknesses and the mistakes they have made. Events and behaviours in themselves which people would actually prefer not to think about. Topics that have been discussed before, and which remind them how they attempted in the past, in vain, to learn something or to change something in their own actions.
- Supervision and action learning take place in a group context. Working in a group, however familiar the members are with each other, also involves a certain tension. 'What will "they" think about me if I raise this issue, or make these comments? Will I still belong if I say openly that I sometimes don't really know what to do in a given situation?' 'All the others seem to be very sure of themselves. I still have doubts about the right course of action here, but what will happen if I say so?'

Supervision and action learning clearly arouse ambivalent feelings: they have a valuable and 'fun' side, but also generate feelings of uncertainty and tension. Faced with both pleasant and unpleasant feelings, it is a normal response to take up arms against the latter. This is not always the result of a conscious process. In psychological jargon, the 'weapons' with which one surrounds oneself are called 'defences' (Harrison, 1963; see also Chapter 8 of De Haan and Burger, 2004). Everyone needs defences sometimes and makes use of them; the question is always to what extent, and when. Adulthood presupposes the ability to recognise and accept tension in oneself without immediately reacting 'defensively', unless the situation so requires – in other words, an ability to make a more or less conscious assessment of whether or not to use your defences.

So how do you tell if tensions or unpleasant feelings are present in people or in a group? The following brief list of signs does not claim to be exhaustive!

- Somehow or other, it is difficult to get sessions organised. People don't show up, some cancel – sometimes at short notice – some turn up much too late. Others start off by saying they will have to 'leave a bit earlier' this time.
- Occasionally, it is hard to get sessions off to a purposeful start. Notes have to be compared first; diaries are brought out to arrange an appointment; a tasty anecdote is served up; and of course a couple of people are busying themselves with 'tea or coffee'.
- No one actually has any issues to raise. Someone who had promised to prepare a case stares at the ceiling and says that it didn't 'work out'. The facilitator looks round the room. 'Someone else, perhaps?' Silence. In fact, no one actually has any urgent issues, or issues suitable for this session.
- Sometimes the group seems to lack the patience to explore quietly 'What is the problem and who has the problem?' A hurried atmosphere prevails, with people appearing to know very quickly what 'the' solution should be. Complicated issues are reduced to something that looks extremely simple.
- The conversation simply will not get off the ground – hardly anyone volunteers a contribution; people are passive and expectant.
- Now and then, people raising cases behave in a very exaggerated manner. For example, they can describe a client in very pejorative terms, deny things that everyone can see ('No, I am not angry!!'), hide something that is clear to everyone (such as carelessness, for example), or rationalise away an unpleasant feeling ('No, fortunately the client turned down my proposal – I really didn't feel like getting into that.').

The complicated thing about all of these events is that they may mean both 'something' and 'nothing'. They may mean 'something' in the sense that they are responses to tension or uncertainty. They may also mean 'nothing', in that really no one has any issues to raise, for example; sometimes some people just don't show up, or show up late.

As the facilitator, you will probably develop a growing sensitivity to these tensions – perhaps because a particular atmosphere or certain incidents keep recurring, because it is always the same people who turn up, or because you just get a 'gut feeling'. This might be a good reason to intervene. Yet intervention requires care.

If the behaviour you are observing is a reaction to tension or uncertainty, it has an important and useful function. People are protecting themselves

Figure 13.1 *Handling difficult moments*

against the unpleasant and painful aspects of the group session. There is no need to condemn such behaviour or describe it too harshly. There may be 'something wrong' that you can see and hear, but there may also be 'nothing wrong'. The participants in the session are generally the best people to judge, by asking themselves what may be going on within themselves.

This means that the facilitator does not actually make the diagnosis, because what (s)he thinks or feels is less important than what the participants think and feel. The facilitator may, however, request the participants' attention in order to explore what is happening at a given moment. He or she might say, for example, 'I notice that many people always come late.' Or, 'I notice that there have been a lot of long silences recently.' Or, 'It seems to be difficult to come up with a case.' There may be no difference of opinion within the group about the truth of these observations. Indeed, this may represent a good opportunity to invite feedback (see also the feedback rules in Chapter 10). Rather, the question is what these observations 'mean', and that is precisely what you can ask. For example, 'I notice many people always come late and I wonder why this is.'

Such an open and neutral manner creates an opportunity for people to consider within themselves the actual reason for them coming late. It may be that 'nothing' is wrong – they often arrive late wherever they are; or some people are very busy at present; or some had simply forgotten and remembered at the last minute; or it took longer to get to the meeting place than they had thought.

Perhaps there is 'something' wrong – someone says that (s)he 'finds these sessions difficult' in a number of respects. Whereupon you, as facilitator, can ask what this member's difficulty is, and how others see things. In this way thoughts and feelings may be explored. Exchanging and comparing them can help reduce this uncertainty and tension and create greater intimacy.

To put it briefly, there may be 'nothing' wrong and there may be 'something' wrong. If people say that there is 'nothing' wrong, you as facilitator may doubt this, but often there is little point in challenging this. If this is 'the truth' for the participants, it often makes little sense to try to change people's views by imposing your opinions on them, so to speak. The only thing you can do is draw attention to issues if the phenomenon recurs, again in a neutral manner and possibly with the comment that the group 'has been here before'. This again creates an opportunity for the participants to say something about what your observation means in their eyes.

Summary: handling difficult moments

Difficult moments are
- When it is hard to get sessions organised – people not showing up, cancelling, turning up late, etc.
- When it is hard to get sessions started properly – members talk about other matters, are making arrangements, organising tea and coffee.
- When no one has any issues to raise.
- When the group lacks the patience to explore.
- When the conversation simply will not get off the ground.
- When there is exaggerated behaviour on the part of the issue holder.

Possible cause
- Response to tension or uncertainty – i.e. a protective measure against unpleasant and painful matters.

Possible approach by the facilitator
- Recounting your own observations.
- Asking the participants to explore in themselves what is happening at that moment.

Part III

Learning from experience

*It is only by the constant use of all four instruments,
moving up and down from one to another, that
knowledge of what is in its nature good can be
engendered – and that with difficulty – in a soul
which is itself naturally good.*

(...)

*It is only when these four are rubbed together and
subjected to tests in which questions and answers
are exchanged in good faith and without malice that
finally, when human capacity is stretched to its limit,
a spark of understanding and intelligence flashes out
and illuminates the subject at issue.*

From Plato's Seventh Letter
to Dion of Syracuse

Introduction
Authorities on learning

This theoretical section contains an overview of a number of well-known and relevant learning models. I will try to put those models in the context of a longer tradition. Due to the apparent straightforwardness and applicability of some of the models, these chapters will sometimes give the impression that learning is a well-charted and well-understood phenomenon. This is by no means the case. Learning, like perception, has been one of the last fields to be explored systematically by human inquiry. This delay in scrutinising perception and cognition has resulted precisely from the way they relate to human inquiry itself. Moreover, learning goes to the heart of human behaviour and human information processing and therefore relates to the most complex structure known to man – the human brain.

Because the processes involved in learning are still so poorly understood, the chapters which follow are intended to:

- invite the reader to think about this subject, which is highly relevant to peer consultation
- give the reader a broader framework within which a wide range of learning activities can be placed.

It is not possible, in this theoretical section of the book, to give definitive answers to all questions about learning, simply because there are no definitive answers. Such questions might include the following:

- Learning is based on a paradox which the learner is unable to resolve – how do you know what you have to learn if you haven't learned it yet? How can one arrive autonomously and independently at completely new actions?
- The outcome of learning again rests on a paradox which the learner is unable to resolve – the formulation of a new answer or new knowledge leads both to new insights and experiences as well as to barriers to new insights and experiences, because accepting any answer or model also involves disregarding viewpoints or information which do not conform with it (Armstrong, 2003). So, how do you manage learning in such a way that it helps rather than hinders?

- Learning changes the learner, who actually becomes a different person in the process. How deeply does learning impact on personality? How vulnerable are we where learning is concerned? What is the interaction between our emotions and our capacity for learning?

At the end of the first four chapters in Part III, and of each chapter in Part IV, the reader can follow, as a narrative example, the course of one specific learning experience with colleagues – the collective writing of this book (seen through the eyes of Erik de Haan).

14
Some concepts and definitions

In his much-quoted book *Experiential Learning* (1984), David Kolb describes how a diverse body of learned scholars developed very similar models of learning in the first half of the twentieth century. He shows that the American pragmatic philosopher John Dewey, the German originator of 'T-group' training and organisation development Kurt Lewin, and the Swiss developmental psychologist Jean Piaget – working relatively independently of each other – used the same two polarities with regard to learning, each of them leading to a cyclical learning model with four (virtually identical) phases. These phases are often referred to as 'Kolb's learning styles'. This book also adopts this term and follows Kolb in that the learning styles are not necessarily assumed to follow each other cyclically.

We begin with a number of frequently used definitions which have the advantage that they are operationalised in such a way that they do not refer to the inner world inaccessible to an observer:[1]

- Learning: a process in which knowledge is created by the transformation of experience.[2]
- Knowledge: human knowledge (perceptions, cognitions, skills, attitudes) represents an irreversible change in potential actions.[3]

1. The vital, problem-driven character of learning, as the learner often experiences it personally, is intentionally omitted from these definitions, which describe 'learning' as it can be observed from the outside. We will come back to this aspect of learning in Chapter 18.
2. Dewey (1938) includes in his definition the fact that learning also prepares the learner for new experiences. In this connection he refers to learning from, through and to the experience. So, for Dewey, the definition of learning itself draws attention to the circular nature of learning. This will be emphasised later in this chapter.
3. This definition is based on accepted definitions in research into the interaction between man and his environment ('psychophysics'). For this definition, and further references to other sources for perception and apprehension on the basis of cyclical interaction with our surroundings, see Koenderink (1999).

The following definitions provide clarification of three key terms:

- *Transformation*. Here this applies to appropriation or processing – in the sense of making an experience one's own or finding it applicable.
- *Experience*. In the context of this study this should be interpreted very broadly, such that it also covers reading a book or dreaming. This is why each of the learning styles described below refers to experiential learning – learning is equated in the definition with experiential learning.
- *Action*. This relates to a self-initiated experience, also with a broad scope – having an idea, putting forward an opinion or suppressing a reaction are also actions.

According to many thinkers, there are two polarities of vital importance in learning, both of which have a long tradition in Western learning theory (theory of knowledge, epistemology):

1. *Apprehension versus comprehension.* This distinction[1] relates to the type of knowledge or outcome of learning.
   - *Apprehension* (knowledge of acquaintance) is a direct experience of something – an experience which is both unique and non-transferable. The best advice for someone seeking the same experience is to suggest where they could go and what they might do in order to achieve it. In traditional jargon this is referred to as apprehension. It is a matter of knowing something.
   - *Comprehension* (knowledge about) is being in possession of a fact about something that one can express in language and so can transfer easily. In traditional jargon this is referred to as comprehension. It is a matter of knowing about something.

2. *Internal versus external processing.* This distinction[2] relates to the type of transformation of learning that takes place.

1. Philosophers such as Bertrand Russell and William James have written interestingly about this distinction, which is an ancient one seen, for example, in the ancient Greeks' thinking about knowledge (compare the difference between the Greek words *gnoonai* and *eidenai* or between the French *connaître* and *savoir*). The distinction between apprehension and comprehension is topical at present within the field of 'knowledge management'. Usually a distinction is drawn between implicit and explicit knowledge, where explicit knowledge can be communicated, stored and managed easily. This is much more difficult with implicit knowledge (see, for example, Nonaka and Takeuchi, 1995).
2. Psychologists such as Carl Jung and Jean Piaget have written interestingly about this distinction, which predates the discipline of psychology itself – for example, it may be seen in the difference between the nominalists (*esse in intellectu*) and realists (*esse in re*) of the Middle Ages.

Figure 14.1 *Learning with colleagues can be a very pleasant experience*

- *Internal processing* (introversion, intention) means moving inward to generate knowledge, by concentration and reflection.
- *External processing* (extraversion, extension) means moving outward to generate knowledge, by experimenting and acting.

According to Kolb, it is important to regard these two distinctions not as sliding scales between two poles, but as different polarities in which we can develop at the same time. Combining one type of knowledge with one transformation method in each case gives four different transformations whereby knowledge is arrived at, or four different learning styles.

An example: Erik's diary of *Learning with Colleagues* (1)

Learning how to learn about learning – it's enough to drive you crazy! It is good, but sometimes very confusing, that Dutch, unlike many other languages, uses one word 'leren' to cover both 'teaching' and 'learning'. Good because you yourself learn from teaching others; confusing because learning is a term that can refer to oneself. You learn yourself, you try to help your clients learn, and one day you decide to write down everything you learned in the process, to create texts about learning … and what do you find? Even during the collective writing of those texts, you have all sorts of unexpected experiences from which – very tentatively – you learn. So you learn through learning how to teach about learning!

This example, using the experience of writing this book, consists of eight extracts from a diary that I kept throughout the writing process – a period of over four years. The continuing story of learning during the writing process, it has been trimmed into extracts which are inserted into the various chapters of the last two sections of the book, which deal with learning and learning groups. At the end of each extract I include a short reflection relating to the relevant chapter of *Learning with Colleagues*.

6 November 1996: a cautious beginning

Adrie[1] has an idea for a book and calls us in. He has a title: *Learning with Colleagues*. He has also found a publisher. Heleen and I react positively but with surprise. So now we are to write a book about learning. Ever tackled such a difficult subject? I feel honoured to be invited to do so by an experienced colleague. But I do wonder why, exactly, and for the time being I decide to view it primarily a good way of getting some more experience of facilitating learning groups.

Within a week we receive a huge pile of reading material from Adrie. Now the motivation is starting to wear off a bit. Ever thought learning could be so dull? And what a terribly wide subject area 'learning' is – how long will it take to become an expert in this field? We meet regularly in the following months and produce short texts for each other. The difficult thing for me is that 'learning' is a catch-all term, covering everything and nothing. I am reminded of a session a few years previously with a consultant who started by asking us what we actually wanted to learn from him. The question threw us into confusion. I came up with a paradoxical answer: 'Could you do something with me for a minute without teaching me anything?' He came over to me, shook my hand and played a dressing-

---

1. The full names of the colleagues mentioned in this diary are Adrie van den Berge, Heleen Bruining and Ina Ahuis. I am very grateful to them for their support in publishing this diary.

up game with me that lasted one minute – he put some sunglasses on me, undid the buttons on my shirt one by one and did them up again, and so on. It was a unique experience for me. Tension was generated between us – a tension that made the moment meaningful, and therefore perhaps instructive for us both ... at least in showing how difficult it is *not* to learn.

Some concepts and definitions explained

Sometimes you need definitions when you start to learn something. My learning from this book is starting in a very unstructured way. I am not actually sure what I am being asked to do. It's strange how many definitions of learning leave out the idea of a problem and of the need to learn – in fact, just like the manner in which I started this book. Learning seems to be able to take place in the absence of any problem that is really bothering you. In this case it starts with a tempting invitation from a highly esteemed colleague.

Summary: concepts and definitions of learning

Learning occurs between the following polarities:
1. *Apprehension*: being familiar with, in direct experience, versus comprehension: being aware of, with factual explanation.
2 *Internal processing* (processing inwardly what you learn) versus *external processing* (applying or experimenting with what you learn).

Learning occurs as a process within and between these polarities and the result of that process is that you accumulate *knowledge*.

The accumulation of knowledge means that you can *transform* the experiences you gain into new options for action – in other words, these experiences give rise to *change*.

Learning is a largely *irreversible* process – you cannot un-learn something. You can, of course, distance yourself from what you have learned, but that changes you as well, and therefore is in itself also learning!

15
Four learning styles

This chapter follows the description of Kolb's learning styles in his book *Experiential Learning* (1984). Kolb bases his model on the pairs of terms introduced in the previous chapter:
- apprehension versus comprehension (the type of 'knowing')
- internal processing versus external processing (the type of 'transformation').

Figure 15.1 *Transformation of experiences takes place in a variety of ways*

The types of knowing and transformation are summarised below along a vertical and a horizontal axis respectively, together with the four terms used by Kurt Lewin (1951) in his model (Figure 15.2).[1]

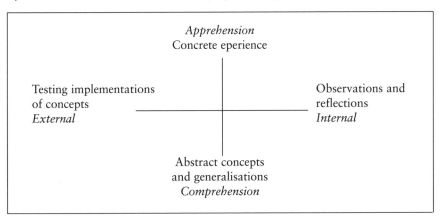

Figure 15.2 *Learning occurs between two pairs of polarities*

Combining the 'ways of knowing' and 'transformations' two by two gives the four familiar learning styles in the four quadrants of Figure 15.2. Several decades of research in this field have shown that scores on the different learning styles are independent and say something about individual learning preferences. (See Appendix D for the 'Learning style inventory', which can be used to assess personal learning styles.)

The four learning styles will be used here as a sort of stepping-stone for different ways of learning. Figure 15.3 offers an introduction, with an example to illustrate each learning style.

1. Interestingly, Dewey developed the same model back in 1910 and applied it to self-managed learning in 1938 (see Chapter 8). Dewey strongly emphasised the learners' participation in developing an objective ('purpose') in order to manage their own learning activities. When learners participate in this, according to Dewey they will first experience an initial impulse or desire to learn (top of the diagram), then a period of observing and reflecting on the situation (top right-hand side), then coordinate their observations with knowledge from memory or information sources (bottom) before moving on to opinion-forming (bottom right-hand side). Only after completing this path will learners be able to take purposeful action in order to gain new experiences (bottom left). Piaget (1970) used a similar diagram in his research into human development from infant to adolescent. According to him, development starts at the top left with active experimentation. Piaget describes the sensorimotor phase (age 0–2 years). This is followed by the representative phase (2–7 years) at the top right, the specific operations and systematic thinking phase (8–11 years) at the bottom right, and finally the formal operations and hypothesis testing phase (12–15 years) at the bottom left.

Apprehension

4. Accommodation   1. Divergence
'Doing'   'Observing'

External   *Internal*
processing   *processing*

3. Convergence   2. Assimilation
'Applying'   'Analysing'

Comprehension

Figure 15.3 *Kolb's four learning styles (1984)*

a. Divergence

In this learning style you consider specific situations from many different perspectives and establish links between different aspects and approaches. Besides listening and looking carefully, your imagination and powers of observation help you to consider events, issues or problems from a variety of angles. This is a divergent learning style because you keep seeing new aspects, which keep leading to new meanings and values (Figure 15.4).

Figure 15.4 *A* Dutch *proverb says: 'Not even a donkey trips over the same stone twice.' Here is how that is possible for the divergent donkey*

This learning style is especially suited to the appropriation of new experiences and the generation of new ideas. It is often accompanied by interest in, and sensitivity to, personal and interpersonal aspects.

An example
Consider learning arising from an intensive and difficult day at work. At home, the professional tells his partner how it all went, what he did and when, and who responded to it and how. His partner listens with warmth and understanding and adds some observations of her own about the colleagues concerned. After five minutes' talking and listening, the professional's problems appear to be much more straightforward and easier to resolve than he first thought.

b. Assimilation

In this learning style you accommodate diverse observations and reflections in an integrated explanation or in theoretical models. Using precise and sharp logic, you judge information and models on their merits. This is an assimilative learning style, because you assimilate diverse ideas and information or adapt them to an encompassing theoretical framework (Figure 15.5).

Figure 15.5 *Not even the assimilative donkey trips over the same stone twice*

This learning style is especially suited to the inclusion of data in models and the design of experiments to test those models. The interest here is mainly in the beauty and completeness of the models themselves, possibly at the expense of interest in people or in practical matters.

An example

Consider the learning of new information in one's own specialist field. The professional buys a book, attends a lecture or asks colleagues exactly what those new developments are about, then summarises the new literature and relates it to models with which (s)he is already familiar.

c. Convergence

In this learning style, theory and practice are combined in achieving practical and achievable solutions. Using selective attention, problem-solving capabilities and progress-oriented decision-making, you adapt and apply models in order to provide new answers and solutions to practical questions. This is a convergent learning style, because the style helps you get to grips with complexity and ambiguity and transform them into a single, defensible approach (Figure 15.6). This learning style is therefore well suited to situations where a single correct answer or solution is necessary and possible. Concentrated attention and the nerve to break new ground and take decisions often go hand-in-hand with this learning style.

Figure 15.6 *Not even the convergent donkey trips over the same stone twice*

An example
The situation just after the end of an educational programme – the professional has her diploma in the bag, has passed in all the subjects relevant to her area of work and so is sufficiently well-versed in the subject matter. Now she has to decide where to apply this knowledge. She has to find her niche in the complex and intricate employment market. In deciding where to work, she selects those aspects of her profession that are most relevant to her and becomes acquainted with day-to-day practice in her new field.

d. Accommodation

In this learning style you can achieve practical results by rolling up your sleeves, trying things out and seeking out new experiences. Using adaptability, commitment and entrepreneurship, you take steps to follow up choices and try out solutions. This is an accommodative learning style, because you adapt and react to changing circumstances (Figure 15.7). This learning style is particularly suited to complex situations in which progress is required, and thus well suited to a 'trial-and-error' approach. A person's interest is often intuitive and implicit, directed towards action, influence, mastery and new experiences.

Figure 15.7 *Not even the accommodating donkey trips over the same stone twice*

An example
Consider learning particular driving manoeuvres, such as turning or parallel parking – theory and your own reflections are both abundant, and yet irrelevant to the demands of the situation. It is now a matter of mastering the sequence of movements through extensive practice.

Two complementary polarities can also be distinguished in the four learning styles:[1]

1. Who adapts: the context, or we ourselves?
In assimilation and accommodation, the question is who adapts. Do we adapt a vast array of incomplete and perhaps unreliable data to our models, or are we prepared to adapt ourselves to that complex environment? When accumulating knowledge, do we consider general ideas and theories or the particular, the special, the individual?

2. Where is the attention focused: plurality or unity?
Divergence and convergence relate to the assessment of the aspects of reality which are under consideration. Do we seek out the richness of a plurality of meanings or do we attempt to create unity from the apparent diversity and ambiguity, in order to be able to proceed to action? The process of learning in the different dimensions is expressed in Figure 15.8. The non-closure of the curved arrows indicates the change or transformation which is always associated with learning.[2] The change in the diagram need not always be

1. The reader may recognise old philosophical questions in these polarities – questions which divided philosophers such as Plato and Aristotle, or Parmenides and Heraclitus, and which have played a leading role in the learning and development of Western philosophy:
   - *Assimilation versus accommodation.* Plato, the idealist, was a pre-eminent assimilative thinker, able to bring together many centuries of Greek philosophy in one abstract corpus full of ideas. Aristotle was the first of the modern Greek philosophers and led an active life both as the teacher of Alexander the Great and as a practical scientist. His notes cover the entire spectrum of human inquiry. At a number of points he emphasizes that all true knowledge is knowledge of the particular.
   - *Convergence versus divergence.* Parmenides, in his *Path to the Truth*, sang the praises of the underlying unity of all things. Heraclitus, on the other hand, praised – in intuitive and engaging language – the underlying diversity: 'If all things went up in smoke, it is by smell that we could still distinguish them.'
2. Argyris and Schön propose that structurally different learning processes are possible, namely with a single loop and with a double loop, or first-order and second-order learning (see Chapter 18 and Argyris and Schön, 1978). Higher orders are sometimes proposed as well. These authors derive from system theory or cybernetics (see for example Wiener, 1948) the distinction between linear feedback (first-order, single-loop) and higher orders (double-loop, triple-loop), in which the feedback is non-linear. The classic comparison is with the steering of a ship ('cybernetics' means

incremental – unlearning can also result from learning. The change itself need not always even be conscious.[1]

Figure 15.8 can be used to illustrate the various learning processes accepted by Kolb's learning model.

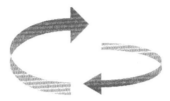

Figure 15.8 *Visualising the process of learning*

e. Singular learning

Singular learning is possible within each of the four learning styles. Kolb (1984) created an extensive classification of learning and development in various professions, and showed how, in most professional education, singular learning takes place, preferably within one learning style. (See also Chapter 19.)

Figure 15.9 offers four examples of singular learning, one for each learning style. Later it will be shown how peer consultation is often a good example of singular learning within the 'divergent' learning style.

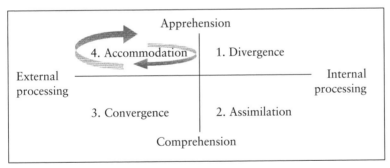

Figure 15.9 *Singular learning*

helmsmanship), where we can distinguish between course corrections influencing the orientation of the ship with respect to the desired course, and course changes due (for example) to sudden alterations in weather conditions. Within the definitions chosen here, the distinction between single-loop and double-loop learning is irrelevant, since we see learning as an irreversible change and single-loop transformations, by definition, are not that. In addition, the Argyris and Schön theory relates primarily to the level of intervention appropriate to reflection, which means that they are writing mainly about divergent learning.

1. See, for example, Polanyi's book on tacit or automatic learning (1966). Unconscious unlearning is 'forgetting'.

f. Dual learning

It is also possible to alternate between two adjacent learning styles during learning. This means that four learning processes are possible in turn (Figure 15.10).

Generally speaking, this form of learning is more robust than singular learning because we:

- either coordinate the inner and outer world, or
- anchor 'comprehension' in 'apprehension'.

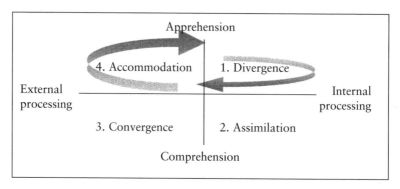

Figure 15.10 *Double-loop learning*

> *An example*
> Kolb cites the example of learning a language, other than from schoolbooks. You start by listening carefully and thinking about what you have heard. Then you try to join in and say the words you have heard, preferably at the right times. This gives rise to a cyclical process in which you learn to speak better and better in the foreign language. As long as no grammar interferes and as long as you yourself do not construct any theories – using your knowledge of other languages, for example – the learning process takes place entirely within the two learning styles (divergent and accommodative) indicated in Figure 15.10, both of which remain close to the specific experience. The pre-eminent example is therefore learning a language for the first time, at a very young age – when no 'comprehension' interferes!

Triple learning is impossible, not only because we would cross the diagonal but also because we would be using all of the axes and so (albeit to a tiny extent) be using the fourth learning style. I will return to 'crossing the diagonal' in Chapter 18, about project-based action learning, and look at attempts to blend the opposite learning styles in double-loop learning.

g. The full cycle of experiential learning

This is the full learning cycle, which moves from a new experience to a full development in practice and theory, internally and externally, and so on to the next new experience.

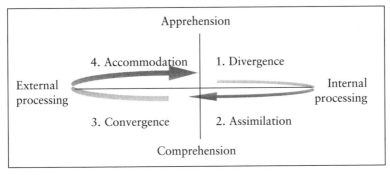

Figure 15.11 *The learning cycle*

An example
This example starts with the discovery of a new face at a meeting at work. You wonder who this new person is (divergence) – a new colleague or a visitor? Perhaps you ask yourself which new colleagues you are still expecting (assimilation) and decide, for example, that this might be the one who is due to start work next month (convergence). You go up to the stranger (accommodation), test your assumption and quickly get into conversation with an exchange of various experiences – which, of course, gets you thinking again (divergence)!

An example
Another example is the classical scientific enterprise that starts with a phenomenon, moves on to reflection on it (divergence), to forming a theory (assimilation), to formulating a hypothesis (convergence), to testing the hypothesis (accommodation), to new phenomena, to new reflection, and so on.

The full learning cycle cannot be travelled in the opposite direction. However, starting from a specific experience both directions are equally valid. Kolb uses the example of a rose which he finds unexpectedly on his desk, with the following possible reactions:

• divergent: 'Who put that there?!' or
• accommodative: picking up the rose, smelling it, placing it in a glass of water.

The convergent learning style has a preferred direction – from knowledge to action, from options to decision-making. As a result, an 'accommodative' start leads to the completion of the learning circle in the direction outlined above. The other learning styles also have a preferred direction to some extent: divergence is directed inwards, assimilation is directed at comprehension and accommodation at new experiences.

An example: Erik's diary of *Learning with Colleagues* (2)

18 April 1997: the first deadlock
Today we have another appointment with our writing group. The appointment was originally scheduled from 9 to 3 o'clock. Now, however, I have made another appointment with a client until 11, so we have agreed that I will join them later. Around 11 I ring them and say that I will be another half hour or so, and then don't show up until 12.30! Adrie and Heleen are clearly annoyed and disappointed, and rightly so. After lunch we start talking. 'We're at a standstill, we don't want to go on. None of us is doing anything. Why are we actually writing this book? Aren't there enough books about learning already?' Heleen and I seek instructions from Adrie. What exactly is the book to be about? Who is to take which role? Isn't our knowledge of 'learning', and thus our possible individual contributions, far too diverse? Can I really feel involved? Is this really my project?

Adrie holds us to our agreement, which implies a commitment to make an effort and devote time to the book. 'And if it doesn't become your own we will have to stop, and I'll continue in some other way.' I myself have the feeling that I don't have much to offer; indeed, I notice that I prefer to work on other texts these days ... But right from the outset I thought it was an attractive and instructive project, I enjoyed every minute I managed to spend on it. So I am keen to go on, but also have doubts about the eventual outcome. Again I say that I am committed to the project, and indeed that my commitment is represented by my writing this diary about it, which I do the very same day. Yes, the diary is continuing, but as far as the book is concerned we are well and truly at a standstill ...

Four learning styles
I am now actually creating the problem that was absent at the start of our learning experience: by approaching the task half-heartedly, turning up late to appointments, not writing very much, not displaying ownership, and so on. Without such a problem, I find I am not sufficiently involved – but with my 'problematic' presence I am at risk of thwarting our collaboration. It is the age-old problem encountered during the initial phases of group development. Do I belong here? Do I take responsibility? Can I express myself in this new group? Provided we face up to it, this problem can generate the creative tension that is needed if we are to produce something together and continue to learn ourselves.

At this time all three of us are feverishly searching for a conceptual framework within which we can place our writing. Heleen and I are writing pieces on 'my way of learning' independently of each other, in the hope that it will give us something to go on. In terms of learning style, I find that Adrie and I are quite similar, both of us feeling particularly at home in the assimilative learning style. Heleen seems to be more of an accommodator, because she often wants to get down to work right away.

Summary: four learning styles

The meeting of the polarities 'apprehension versus comprehension' and 'internal processing' versus 'external processing' gives rise to four different learning styles. These styles, in turn, are also complementary in pairs.
- From apprehension to internal processing: *divergence*.
- From internal processing to comprehension: *assimilation*.
- From comprehension to external processing: *convergence*.
- From external processing to apprehension: *accommodation*.

Learning takes place both within and between the learning styles. A total of nine processes of knowledge accumulation can be distinguished:

Singular
1. Divergent.
2. Assimilative.
3. Convergent.
4. Accommodative.

Dual
5. Divergent and assimilative.
6. Assimilative and convergent.
7. Convergent and accommodative.
8. Accommodative and divergent.

Full cycle
9. Divergent —→ assimilative —→ convergent —→ accommodative —→ divergent.

The full cycle is also known as the learning circle or learning spiral.

16
Learning to learn better

The previous chapter introduced a learning model that provides a comprehensive description of human learning behaviour and appears in the literature in many forms.[1] We can now go one level of abstraction higher – how can we improve the quality of learning? Learning itself often represents an improvement in quality ('creation of new knowledge'), so improving the quality of learning is a matter of the 'quality of quality', or learning to learn.

The authorities on learning have different views on how to improve the efficiency and effectiveness of learning – in other words, how to achieve improvement both in learning things right and in learning the right things. Different researchers write very different, and sometimes contradictory, things about improving the quality of learning, however. I do not intend to get involved in this controversy here, merely to discuss three aspects that many people believe to be important in learning:
1. learning about learning itself – meta-learning
2. self-managed learning
3. facilitating learning.

1. Meta-learning

If we look at specifically human aspects of learning, our capacity to 'learn about learning' is particularly striking. Take, for example, this book – and Chapter 15 in particular. If it hits the mark, the reader may feel encouraged to think about learning, and to apply the divergent learning style to learning

---

1. See, for example, Honey and Mumford, 1986, and Nonaka and Takeuchi, 1995. The 'knowledge spiral' of Nonaka and Takeuchi is virtually identical to the four-style model discussed here. However, it is difficult to recognise at first because the knowledge spiral is rotated by 135° compared with Kolb's model, so that assimilative learning (referred to as 'dialogue') comes at the top of the spiral, convergent ('linking knowledge') on the right, accommodative ('learning by doing') at the bottom and divergent ('building the field') on the left. They also distinguish between apprehension and comprehension – 'tacit knowledge' and 'explicit knowledge'.

itself. We can also apply the convergent learning style to learning – for example, by deciding to set the book aside at this point and first planning what to do with the material in it. Or the assimilative learning style, by comparing the theory under discussion with our own theoretical baggage or by developing learning theories ourselves. Finally, we might draw upon the accommodative learning style, by embarking together with colleagues on a search for new forms of learning, such as training, coaching, literature study, and so on.

In general, it is thought that learning about learning, particularly by the reflective (divergent) route, is conducive to learning – see, *inter alia*, Schön (1983). By constantly monitoring learning, we can perhaps improve the quality of learning. Effective learning involves a continual switching between learning itself and thinking about learning. A high regard for meta-learning results in the recommendation that learning objectives be made explicit, and readjusted during learning. Learning goals and learning objectives encourage learners to think about their own learning. However, one may also have doubts about the effectiveness of meta-learning in some circumstances, precisely because it distracts from learning itself. Polanyi (1966), for example, argues for an unconscious form of (predominantly accommodative) learning (tacit learning), which calls for considerable concentration and involvement, and may therefore be disrupted by activities at the meta-level.

2. Self-managed learning

Self-managed learning can be seen as the next step beyond meta-learning. Here, the learner uses the information generated by meta-learning to manage his or her own learning, to take decisions about which learning activity or learning style is the most appropriate. By managing one's own learning, the learner assumes greater responsibility for it.

Two objections may be raised against self-managed learning:

- It is based on a paradox – how can the person learning know what (s)he still has to learn? Until this has been achieved, the learner will therefore have to leave the managing to someone else – or to the demands of his or her circumstances.
- Autonomy is not always helpful when it comes to acquiring new information. To that end, it is often important to trust and rely on the greater knowledge and experience of others.

We will return to this subject at greater length in Chapter 22.

3. Facilitating learning

Here, I would like to look at the role of facilitator more broadly than in Part II. That section was concerned with facilitating peer consultation, while the present one deals more generally with the facilitation of all forms of learning.

What should a facilitator of learning – a teacher – do within each learning style in order to encourage and support learning? It is helpful if the facilitator chooses behaviour that fits in with the given learning style, so as to support the learner by 'setting the right example':

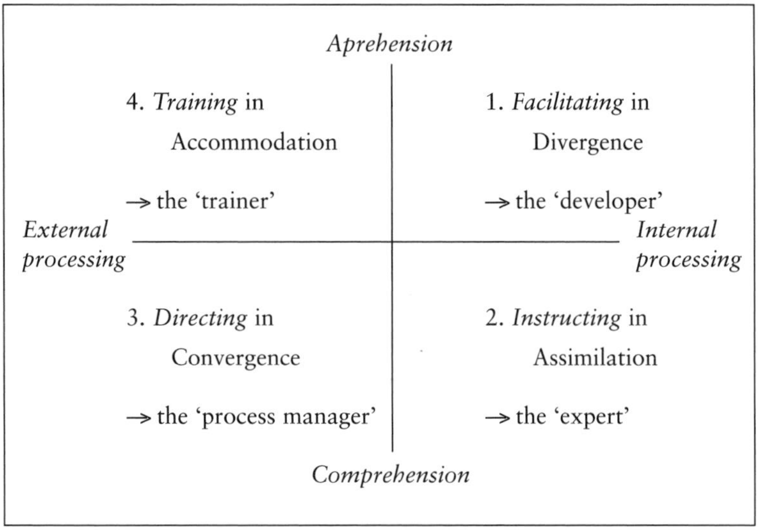

```
                            Aprehension
                                |
    4. Training in              |        1. Facilitating in
       Accommodation            |           Divergence
                                |
       → the 'trainer'          |           → the 'developer'
External _____|_____ Internal
processing                      |                          processing
                                |
    3. Directing in             |        2. Instructing in
       Convergence              |           Assimilation
                                |
       → the 'process manager'  |           → the 'expert'
                                |
                            Comprehension
```

Figure 16.1 *Facilitator's behaviour appropriate to each of the four learning styles*

The roles of developer, expert and process manager are essentially consulting roles, where the facilitator supports the learner as a client in different ways (de Haan, 2003):

- The *developer* focuses predominantly inwards, on developing the learner personally, and attempts to contribute to this by redefining problems, providing insight into patterns of behaviour and proposing alternatives.
- The *expert* focuses predominantly on content and subject matter, and attempts to contribute by means of analysis, contributing his or her own knowledge and experience and answering questions on the basis of his or her own concepts and methods.
- The *process manager* focuses predominantly on the progress of learning, and approaches to it, and on attempts to create conditions for arriving at a solution – by bringing people together, by making roles explicit and by forcing a decision.

The fourth role is less a consultative and more a strongly participative and encouraging role (de Haan, 2003):

- The *trainer* focuses predominantly on action and entrepreneurship, and contributes primarily by creating situations in which the learner can experiment.

Each of the four facilitation roles reflects the behaviour and activities of the learner himself. Each of them may be used by a facilitator to make these learning activities more effective and efficient. In so doing, facilitators contribute their own knowledge, skill and experience as appropriate to the learning style in question. In other words:

- in the case of the developer, mainly feedback and reflection – i.e. 'people knowledge'
- in the case of the expert, mainly expertise and subject-matter knowledge
- in the case of the process manager, mainly experience in achieving progress and establishing approaches, i.e. experiential knowledge
- in the case of the trainer, mainly nerve and skill in the field of action, experimental and learning situations, i.e. 'action knowledge'.

In general, however, I would expect a good facilitator to do more than simply facilitate the learning itself. A facilitator must know what he or she is doing – in any case (s)he must have more of an idea than the learner. I therefore also expect a facilitator to be able to 'meta-learn' and manage the learning process.

This means that a good facilitator is also able – possibly together with the learner – to investigate whether the learner is working in the most appropriate learning style. A facilitator should also ask, and in some situations judge personally, whether learners:

Figure 16.2 *How can we bring the four different learning styles together?*

- are taking sufficient personal responsibility for their own learning
- have the courage to take the plunge and embark upon new experiments (especially in convergence and accommodation)
- put themselves to the test sufficiently in developing and accumulating knowledge (especially in divergence and assimilation).

This responsibility for learning in a deeper sense also means that the facilitator will choose behaviour other than what fits in with the learning style in use at the time, in order to help the learner move on to a different learning style which might fit better with the current learning process.

It is therefore possible to distinguish the following tasks for which the facilitator can assume responsibility:

- helping the learner within the learning style in question, by choosing the appropriate role
- 'propelling' the learner towards a new learning style, if the facilitator deems this necessary on the basis of his or her own knowledge and skill
- raising the question of the learning itself, and thereby initiating meta-learning.

Now that the role of facilitator has been outlined, I can provide a more detailed overview of Kolb's four learning styles, as shown in Figure 15.3.

An example: Erik's diary of *Learning with Colleagues* **(3)**

23 December 1997: end of our writing collaboration
We experience several months of gradually increasing activity. In particular, I remember one session in the hotel 'The Philosopher', where we designed a 'learning model' of our own. Then the collaboration stalls again. We have been working for over a year now without producing anything we consider suitable for publication. In addition, I am finding it very difficult to 'find a voice' in this group. In the role of 'pupil' I usually can. Then I listen and read the articles handed out to me, and can frequently connect the interesting concepts and ideas to my own experiences out loud. In the role of 'teacher', however, I find it much more difficult. For example, when I am talking about my Ph.D. thesis, which was also largely about learning within the field of psychophysics, the study of human perceptions and actions in interaction with physical changes in the environment. Or when I am talking about the epistemological literature that I read earlier, during my studies. At times like that something painful occurs. I notice that my colleagues are not very interested in these abstract concepts and strange experiences. This makes me uncertain – what can I teach these colleagues? And are they prepared to reconcile themselves, albeit temporarily, to taking on the role of my pupil?

   In the end, our collaboration comes to a stop. Adrie is giving up, and doesn't believe in it any more. I feel angry and disappointed to hear of

	1 Divergence	2 Assimilation	3 Convergence	4 Accommo-dation
What you learn	Experiences, situations, people, ideas	Facts, reflections, observations, models	Facts, theories, results, approaches	Experiences, consequences of choices, actions
How you learn	Inwards, with imagination, sensitivity, observation and reflection	Inwards, with subordination, integration and logic	Outwards, with selective attention, problem-solving, decision-making and focus	Outwards, with adaptability, commitment and entrepreneurship
	'Observing'	'Analysing'	'Initiating'	'Doing'
Examples	Brainstorming Peer consultation	Study Literature research	Multiple choice test Planning	Training Trial-and-error
Meta-learning	Thinking about learning itself*	Testing what has been learned against theory	Measuring and assessing progress (e.g. by audit or examination)	Trying out different learning styles
Facilitator	'Developer' (facilitating)	'Expert' (teaching)	'Process manager' (directing)	'Trainer' (training)
Facilitator's contribution	Feedback and reflection	Expertise and subject-matter knowledge	Progress and alternative approaches	Action and new experiences

* See Argyris and Schön's 'model II learning' (1978).

Figure 16.3 *Overview of Kolb's four learning styles*

the end of our collaborative relationship, but not enough to make an effort to save it. Now our dealings with each other are confined to client projects again, so they are more specific and with reasonably well-defined results. This is much better, as we complement each other much better this way.

Learning to learn better

Gradually more and more problems arise – problems which might perhaps serve as a basis for learning. Problems concerning our roles within the team and regarding the quality of our own learning process. We try to work as equals but miss a (possibly alternating?) facilitator of our learning process. Our thoughts about the collaboration and our ideas concerning the development of each other's texts are becoming less and less productive – perhaps because none of us really wants to invest in this collaboration, and because each of us is already busy enough trying to work together effectively with our clients …?

Summary: learning to learn better

In order to improve learning – to make it more efficient and more effective – it is important to:

- be able to learn in the field of learning itself ('meta-learning')
- manage one's own learning if necessary ('self-managed learning')
- work with an able facilitator during the learning process.

What can be expected of a good facilitator?

- Role behaviour and contribution appropriate to the learning style in question:
  - facilitating in the case of divergence – contribution: feedback and reflection
  - instructing in the case of assimilation – contribution: expertise and subject-matter knowledge
  - directing in the case of convergence – contribution: progress and approach
  - training in the case of accommodation – contribution: action and new experiences
- Being able to *propel the learner* forward towards a different learning style if necessary
- *Initiating and participating in learning about learning* (meta-learning).

17
Upward spirals:
life-long learning

Only by continuing to learn are we able to find answers to changing circumstances and new questions. This is why life-long learning is considered to be of increasing importance in most organisations, of all kinds. In order to remain 'professional', professionals must constantly develop within their own professional practice. It is therefore useful to take a look at long-term learning – the processes that occur when we consider certain questions intensively over a long period.

Following on the model with four learning styles that learners can develop independently, Kolb (1984) proposes a 'multilinear' long-term development of learning. Development is possible within each learning style and is relatively independent of development within the other styles.[1]

Kolb's model distinguishes three developmental phases within each learning style, whereby learners strive for an ever-greater balance between themselves and an increasingly complex environment, so becoming increasingly flexible and freer in terms of their possible answers to questions posed by the environment.[2] In order to achieve this, progress within each learning style occurs in ever-closer relationship with progression within the other styles. It is possible, however, to revert or 'regress' to an earlier phase.

Kolb's three phases are as follows:
1. *Acquisition*: from birth to adolescence.[3] In the acquisition phase a structure develops within which the child can increasingly see itself, and

1. Those who take as their basis the completion of the full learning circle opt, on the other hand, for a simple, linear development of learning. One example is Piaget, who shows in his fundamental studies on developmental psychology that we all travel the learning circle precisely once between birth and the age of fifteen (Piaget, 1970). A more recent example is the book by Nonaka and Takeuchi (1995), where the same learning spiral is travelled again and again.
2. See also Carl Rogers' developmental model (1958).
3. Within this phase, the previously mentioned developmental model of Piaget (1970) is applicable, which therefore adds four 'sub phases' corresponding to an initial development within Kolb's learning styles.

FIgure 17.1 *The riddle of the Sphinx: 'What creature with only one voice walks first on four legs, then on two, and finally on three?'*

behave, as an autonomous entity separate from its environment. As a result, its freedom increases from 'undifferentiated immersion' to 'having a good understanding of its own limitations'.

2. *Specialisation*: adulthood. Growth towards an ever-greater correspondence between personal characteristics and the demands of the environment, by means of training and socialisation in one given direction within one given context. In the specialisation phase an understanding of individuality and competence develops.

3. *Integration*: personal development and fulfilment.[1] During the specialisation phase one learning style often develops at the expense of the others, giving rise to an imbalance. Finding development and expression for the other learning styles is central here, leading to the realisation of harmony and balance.

A whole series of hierarchical learning models can be linked to this developmental model. The phases described above fit in well with the following three approaches to learning in industrial organizations (Simons, 2000):

1. This is Jung's 'individuation' phase (Jung, 1921). Jung says that by no means everyone reaches this phase, and that an existential conflict is often necessary in order to break out of a successful specialisation and to achieve a balance with previously suppressed adaptation abilities (or, in the words of this book, less developed learning styles) at a higher level.

- Traveller's approach – formal learning under the guidance of a 'conventional' facilitator who transfers knowledge and experience. The learner does not participate in meta-learning and does not manage his/her learning personally.
- Trekker's approach: experiential learning, in which learning is a by-product of more autonomous activity guided by the circumstances or by a facilitator. The learner is now a specialist and moves closer to meta-learning.
- Journalist's approach: fully self-managed learning in which the learner is responsible for his/her own learning process and manages it personally.

These increasing degrees of initiative and responsibility on the part of the learner will be revisited in Chapters 20-22, in a number of extensions to peer consultation – short-cycle learning, project-based action learning and self-managed learning.

An example: Erik's diary of *Learning with Colleagues* (4)

24 April 1998: a reader on peer consultation
Adrie and Heleen are carrying out an assignment for a large consultancy which has explicitly requested a reader on learning with colleagues – the consultancy wants to set up a system of peer supervision and action learning for its own consultants. Together Adrie and Heleen draw up an excellent reader, in which they explain methods and examine the role of the facilitator, the art of giving feedback and the pre-conditions for creating the right learning environment.

I notice that I am envious of the other two members of our original team who are now producing such fine results. Fortunately, I am far too busy to worry about it much. My own working practice consists increasingly of peer consultation – participating in action learning, facilitating consultation groups, fitting in peer consultation with long-term learning, and so on.

Upward spirals: life-long learning
My practice is gradually leading me to specialise in the field of 'learning'. I am immersing myself in it, without being able to read too many books or articles about it, and without being able to write about it. In the course of this year I am facilitating consultation groups almost on a weekly basis. Slowly but surely I am becoming a specialist, which will later enable me to take the literature on board much more critically. It is a relief to forget about the idea of a book for almost two years.

Summary: upward spirals

Kolb's developmental model for long-term learning has three phases:
1. Acquisition.
2. Specialisation.
3. Integration.

This is a hierarchical model of long-term learning with increasing:
1. Flexibility.
2. Personal responsibility.
3. Autonomy.
4. Self-management.

18
Downward spirals: fantasies and limitations

The previous chapters looked at learning in as detached and objective a manner as possible, and asked questions such as:
- What is 'learning', really?
- What are the different ways of learning?
- How can learning processes be facilitated?
- And what does learning look like in the long term?

But this did not tell the whole story – indeed, it may have left out a crucial part. The story has not been told from the inside. What does learning actually mean to the learner? Answers to that question are less than comforting – we have all experienced, since our first steps in the world, how sensitive and frustrating learning can be. This chapter considers the unpalatable and disturbing experiences that confront learners.

The unpalatable aspects of learning are something that we easily lose sight of in our optimism or naivety. We try to tell ourselves that learning is good, and constructive, and useful, and that it can only improve us. And we reinforce each other in that view. In most organisations learning has an appealing, 'trendy' connotation. Stories about accelerating changes inside and around our organisations, competitive advantages acquired through intellectual capital, knowledge management and the strength of 'learning organisations', are now so widely told and retold that everyone is participating in work-related learning in one way or another, whether by consulting with a personal coach, attending training courses and seminars, or learning with colleagues in peer consultation, project-based action learning or self-managing networks.

The unpalatable face of learning

I believe that many professionals, including myself, are often stubborn and obstinate – if we are frank about it – when it comes to learning, and also that we are finding it harder and harder to face up to this. Learning has become a 'commodity' for many people – something that is part of the package, that confers status, that requires permanent attention, that you describe each year in your 'personal development plan', and is actually 'a lot of fun' to take part in. Learning is a must! Learning is fun! You put together your own learning menu, seek out inspiring people with whom you feel at ease, or set your heart on activities that give you a 'kick'. You enjoy the novelty and variety, and give yourself over to fantasies in which you grow and develop and in which you are permanently busy becoming a better person.

However, we assume all too easily that we can acquire all kinds of knowledge and skills – that we can develop all kinds of talents, that we will be able to learn things such as a sense of responsibility, customer-orientation, creativity, stamina and business ethics and act accordingly – without much difficulty. Seminars that often last only one or two days claim to provide participants with relevant information in these fields. In actual fact, it is very easy for most of us to draw up a list of things that are impossible for us to learn.

Some examples
Some examples of things I will never learn, however much I try:
- I will never learn to recognise a musical chord or key – I just don't have the ear for it.
- I will never learn to talk in a completely different voice or write with a different hand – my mind and body have their limitations.
- I will never learn to manage a larger organisation financially – I simply cannot afford the necessary investment in time and attention for proper training as a financial controller, which might take several years.
- It seems impossible for me to learn to take feedback from my direct colleagues and clients more lightly.
- It seems impossible for me to assume responsibility for the various tasks and roles I am currently letting slip.

It may be a great disappointment to conclude that learning either does not just happen by itself, or that learning just doesn't happen at all – or, even if it appears to take place, that it makes no difference in the workplace, or even leads to a deterioration in performance. It may be a great disillusionment, too, to have to conclude that bravely carrying on 'learning' in such circumstances gives rise to existential questions and leads to the disconcerting feeling of 'having already tried everything but still getting nowhere'.

I would not have stayed in this field had I not believed passionately that people can learn things and that, by learning, they can sometimes undergo important changes that will better equip them for the tasks facing them, and give them a more positive approach to them. However, I am convinced that changes of this kind within individuals are still very rare and require personal courage and perseverance, no less so than before the 'learning hype' in which so much learning is advertised as being easy and fun. Moreover, learning is not fun – at least not for me. The few real changes that I myself have undergone were accompanied by almost unbearable doubts, pain and depressing questions to which I had no answer.

Reflecting on this at greater length, I have to admit that learning does not have an antithesis – whatever you do, learning always adds to your experiences and thus expands your knowledge. It therefore appears that learning always takes place in some superficial way. If every new experience, every seminar with every teacher, and every reflection on day-to-day work can be called a 'learning activity', nothing is outside the scope of learning. And nothing changes about the things that are so difficult to get to grips with. Those things become even more disturbing – if that is possible – because all our learning activities and our belief in a 'positive attitude' have led us to think that we can learn anything, after which we are forced to admit that we have still stayed the same. We may have had a new experience, but we have not become different, let alone better, as a result.

Forgetting and 'unlearning' are not really opposites of learning, because they too can bring about a change in available knowledge and, as such, can often represent ways of learning something. Or they can be interpreted as 'unsuccessful learning experiences', as a result of which we 'learned something anyway'.

If we frequently find ourselves stymied or confused by these issues, and become disappointed with our own ability to learn, two fairly counter-cultural – and perhaps also unorthodox – assertions start to become increasingly relevant, because they attack head-on the fantasies and constraints which an orientation towards learning can entail:

1. 'Organising is sometimes directly opposed to learning' (Weick and Westley, 1996). 'Organising' implies that you make choices and adhere to them, apply structures, draw up procedures, follow up arrangements, and so on. These are precisely the sorts of actions that often oppose 'learning', because in doing them one fixates things, makes things more efficient, and then continues to act as one did before. 'Learning' involves making things ambiguous and uncertain; it therefore involves 'disorganising', and taking up time in a manner that does not appear useful and efficient. This means that learning can entail unpredictably high costs which are not defensible from a business economics perspective. Learning often proves destructive for 'learning organisations' – a contradiction in terms from this perspective! – partly because it may lead to the disappearance of successful people, products and services.

2. 'Changing is sometimes directly opposed to learning' (Bion, 1965). You can understand something, grasp something, learn to do something, without undergoing any element of the change that might result in you actually doing it. Learning is in those cases directly opposed to changing. Indeed, some people use learning as one of the most powerful ways of avoiding undergoing a major life change.

By finding opposites to learning in this way, I have 'learned' to put learning into a different perspective and, in the context of peer consultation, to look at other aspects as well. For example: Is it benefiting the organisation? Is anything actually changing?

In this way I hope to obtain a clearer understanding of learning as a last defence against change, of the paradoxical aspects of learning, and of tragic aspects which always play a role in learning or attempts to learn. It is my firm conviction that facilitators of consultation groups should develop sensitivity to irony, to the underlying paradox of 'I'm learning so I don't have to do anything', and to the existential and tragic experiences that arise from in-depth learning. From this perspective, Kolb's optimistic learning circle becomes less and less usable and we become more aware of the downside of learning, the vicious spirals which only generate more frustration, avoidance and double messages.

Attempts to break out of the spirals

First we must distinguish between first-order and second-order – or single-loop and double-loop – learning. Single-loop learning has a much less drastic impact than double-loop learning. Single-loop learning means adding elements to an existing arsenal, or making corrections to our knowledge, attitude and skills. A good example of single-loop learning is getting to know a new organisation, or refining skills on the basis of feedback from others. Double-loop learning means charting a fundamentally new course, declaring existing knowledge unusable and building new frameworks for knowledge from the ground up. Double-loop learning is necessary when we get stuck with a given approach or, for example, when we experience a major change in our career. The painful side of learning comes to the fore in double-loop learning in particular, because we have to abandon existing achievements and acquire unfamiliar knowledge.

Some consultation methods that increase the number of approaches and problem definitions employed (such as the ten-step method) are more oriented towards single-loop learning, while other methods, which seek deeper, unknown motives (such as the dominant-ideas method), are more oriented towards double-loop learning.

In order to break out of the 'vicious' spirals, it is worthwhile considering more closely the most pernicious learning activities imaginable. Since he carried out research in the 1950s into the refined methods of brainwashing in Chinese re-education institutes, Edgar Schein has equated 'double-loop learning' in many publications with 'coercive persuasion' – in other words with a change that takes place only on the basis of an extended and aggressive process of dissociation from old convictions, of influence and control, and of enshrining new beliefs. After the ceasefire in the Korean War in 1953, a group of American psychologists and psychiatrists was sent to South Korea to study released prisoners of war and help them reintegrate into Western society. A considerable number of those POWs were found to have become staunch supporters of Maoist politics and communist doctrines.

Schein, as a social psychologist, was part of the group of researchers. He conducted research in Korea into the methods used on the POWs; his report can be read in *Coercive Persuasion* (Schein, Schneider and Barker, 1961). Later, Schein discovered various examples of coercive persuasion in company training schemes in multinational corporations – such as the compulsory nature of the training, the constant repetition of doctrines, the use of group pressure in activities such as communal singing, and a range of other suggestive working methods. On this basis Schein states later that all learning – including single-loop learning! – occurs under pressure and goes hand in hand with heightened anxiety and feelings of guilt. Whoever can afford to avoid learning will always do so, according to Schein.[1]

The book *Coercive Persuasion* contains a vivid description of historic developments and a detailed dissection of dozens of factors which, when combined, give impressive results – a sincere confession of an 'aberration', followed by a gradual integration into the 'correct' way of thinking. In their description the authors use a classic method developed by Lewin (1951) which describes change in three phases – 'unfreezing', 'changing' and 'refreezing'. Schein's theorising on learning starts with a paradox which makes it impossible to escape feelings of guilt or anxiety. On the one hand there is a fear of changing, and on the other hand a fear of staying the same. This gives rise to the ghastly realisation that you must learn simply in order to survive:[2]

- If we give ourselves over to one fear – the 'fear of learning' – avoidance behaviour results. We will try to suppress any information and avoid any action that confronts us with the fact that we have not yet learned something.
- But if the other fear – the 'survival fear', which is often associated with feelings of despondency and powerlessness – gets the upper hand, we will be forced to make an effort to learn.

---

1. When reversed, this would mean that someone inclined by nature towards feelings of anxiety or guilt, and who is therefore more troubled by uncertainty or a bad conscience, will be more inclined towards learning. This hypothesis is frequently confirmed in my own practice.

2. On page 168 of the novel about an emotional learning disability by Mark Haddon (2003), we find Schein's idea in the form of an elegant formula:

$$F_{total} \approx F_{new\ place} \times F_{here} = C_{person}$$

suggesting that every person has a different constant of how much fear (s)he can bear – and that this constant is made up of two inversely proportional fears: the 'fear of learning' $F_{new\ place}$ and the 'survival fear' F_{here}.

Figure 18.1 *The potato-peeling course is well subscribed this spring; through the use of the brainwashing method, the participants are making good progress*

There are therefore two ways of encouraging people to learn – reducing the fear of learning (for example, by increasing safety or giving explanation and support), and increasing an individual's fear of staying the same (for example by means of sanctions or persuasion). The Chinese prisons in the 1950s proved to be highly developed institutes in the field of the latter form of stimulation. Schein shows that techniques used included the following:

- Shattering existing beliefs and values, enhancing feelings of despair, exerting pressure in order to obtain a 'confession' (as part of 'unfreezing').
- Encouraging self-examination – preferably in groups with more 'advanced' prisoners, supported by identification with an always-available interrogator and teacher (as part of 'changing').
- Providing support to encourage new ways of thinking and cognitive reformulations, making available teaching material, encouraging more public self-analysis and feedback, and rewarding 'good' behaviour with more equable relations with guards and fellow prisoners (as part of 'refreezing').

It is noticeable in this connection that the 'refreezing' phase continues autonomously to a great extent after release, in that ex-prisoners find confirmation of predictions made by interrogators and seek connections with the politically engaged in Western society. Moreover, it is disconcerting to note the many parallels between Schein's findings and the learning activities in which we engage in our 'free' society.

Certain recurring patterns also appear to play a role in learning, such as 'group-think' and 'splitting', which appear to be pre-programmed and therefore seem to occur in virtually all of us. In this connection Schein cites the experiments of Asch (1951), which demonstrate that virtually all subjects deviate from correct answers under group pressure. Whenever we perceive ourselves to be the 'odd man out' in a group of four or more people, the vast majority of us believe that we see what the others see, even if they are clearly mistaken. This effect disappears completely, however, if we have even one supporter in the group. An example of splitting is the gulf demonstrated by Argyris and Schön (1978) between what we think and what we say, which means that we rarely tell others immediately and directly what strikes us about their behaviour. Instead, we appear to opt for a careful way of giving minimal feedback, in the hope that this will allow us to retain the initiative and prevent a mutual loss of face.

Single-loop and double-loop learning can also be applied not only to learning groups as temporary organisations, but also to the organisations to which participants in learning groups belong (March, 1991).

- The organisational variant of single-loop learning is the *exploiting* organisation, which attempts to use the results of learning to achieve ever-greater adaptation, efficiency and optimisation. These are the more reactive 'bureaucracies' in a range of different forms.

- The organisational variant of double-loop learning is the *exploring* organisation, which attempts to stimulate continual innovation through learning with a view to ever more fundamental redefinition, re-organisation or reform. These are the more proactive 'adhocracies' in a range of different forms.

March argues that only when organisational single-loop and double-loop learning are both present to a sufficient extent will the organisation be able to survive. Exploration of new alternatives reduces the extent to which existing expertise can be improved and, conversely, increasing exploitation within existing procedures makes experimenting with new procedures less attractive. In both organisational processes, therefore, there is a self-perpetuating tendency that makes following 'the other process' less attractive. In the end, both bureaucracy and adhocracy will come to a standstill. The bureaucracy will be beset by over-specialisation and become inflexible due to over-optimisation, while the adhocracy will be beset by volatility and become unable to complete or deliver anything in accordance with agreed plans or specifications.

The art of creating the 'learning organisation' appears to involve embracing this contradiction between exploiting and exploring and reconciling the two opposites – if only temporarily – without opting for either alternative. According to Weick and Westley (1996), this is possible through improvisation and by making use of humour. According to them, a high degree of alertness is required because this involves a very delicate equilibrium – even before we know it, we are carried off along one of the self-perpetuating processes of organising, in which we come to grief either in a systematising or optimising way (i.e. exploiting) or a paradigm-changing and framework-expanding way (i.e. exploring).

So what does this mean for learning in peer consultation groups? Here, too, there is a great deal of wrestling with learning, much talking about learning without actually doing any, and a lot of misunderstanding when it comes to listening to new, practicable questions or suggestions. Moreover, there are often self-perpetuating processes which tend to make the session either a rigidly organised 'meeting' or a whimsical, free-wheeling 'brainstorm'. On the one hand the group may be tempted to follow a rigid bureaucratic approach – for example, involving moves to make attendance compulsory. On the other, the group may be attracted by a flexible, ad hoc get-together – for example, conducting the session without any overt method. Both tendencies sometimes even arise at different times within the same learning group – indeed, these learning groups may prove to be the most productive ones. They struggle to keep the two polarities in a dynamic balance and attempt to devote attention to tolerating frustration, on the one hand, and the ability to generate inspiration on the other. In most well-established and productive groups, there is a sublimation of the learning paradox at a higher level, with a recurring, painful and unstable opposition between incisive and stimulating questions, on the one hand, and great compassion and respect for the learner on the other.

Summary: downward spirals

The *unpalatable* aspects of learning are experienced as painfully acute:
- when we have to make an effort to learn;
- when we notice that we are having to give something else up for it;
- when it is simply not working for us; or
- when it makes no difference to the way we act.

Learning in groups and organisations evolves in more painful spirals than simply the positive and upward spiral, in the form of:
- *exploitation*: continuing refining and concentration, and
- *exploration*: breaking through barriers in leaps and bounds.

These two tendencies are the group equivalent of two commonly distinguished forms of learning, namely *single-loop* and *double-loop* learning.

In addition, learning in groups and organisations is characterised by certain patterns:
- *group-think*, which makes it difficult as an individual to hold opinions different from those of the rest of the group
- *splitting* between what we believe and what we say, which makes it difficult to tell others what we are think and also to explore our own opinions.

These painful spirals and patterns appear to be inextricably linked with learning, so it is not realistic to try to escape them here. A better approach appears to be:
- to keep searching for a creative balance between the opposites of exploitation and exploration, and thus
- not to start over-organising, but also not to give up essential preconditions such as openness and safety, and
- to be open to emotions, questions and solutions, with as much compassion and respect as possible.

Part IV

From consultation groups to learning networks

Introduction
The boundaries of peer consultation

In this final section of the book, on practical application, I take what we learned about learning in Part III and return to peer consultation groups. I will discuss from a broader perspective the strengths of peer consultation, its limitations and how those limitations can be dealt with.

I have often noticed, both as a participant and as a facilitator, that peer consultation – in all the diversity described in the first two parts of this book, in varying circumstances and for different groups of both professionals and managers – is an extremely powerful instrument.

During the consultation session participants discuss:
- an event or concern from their own practice
- a professional method or strategy from their own practice, or
- something striking that is happening now in this particular group.

Dominant factors in the consultation include:
- linking reflection to practical situations
- giving and receiving personal feedback
- learning from the connection between behaviour inside and behaviour outside the room
- making professional choices and agreements together with colleagues.

Nevertheless, some relevant factors remain relatively under-exposed within peer supervision and action learning. These include:
- The application of what participants have learned in their practice. The latter remains outside the room and can be discussed only secondarily, as 'there-and-then'.
- The pressure for renewal and change. This comes mainly from inside the participant – peer consultation is more predominantly open and supportive than judgmental or exhorting.
- Providing structure and depth to what has been learned by means of theoretical models and previously developed knowledge. For this participants are dependent upon what happens to be introduced in the

group. In addition, by reflecting on specific experiences and instruments they are not stimulated to seek linkages between what has been learned and the existing literature and body of knowledge.

In fact, peer supervision and action learning are fairly one-sided activities which mainly address one learning style, namely divergence. In my view, this is no reason to regard peer consultation as an inferior learning activity. On the contrary, peer consultation – provided it is carried out properly – is so powerful precisely because it does no more than draw largely on that single learning style. Effective divergence calls for discipline and dedication, and the time to appreciate the many different possible approaches to an issue.

For more experienced learning groups which also want to address other learning styles, this section discusses a number of extensions, as follows:

Chapter 20: *Short-cycle learning*. A way of travelling the full learning circle consciously with colleagues.

Chapter 21: *Project-based action learning*. A way of making the tension between opposite learning styles in learning groups productive.

Chapter 22: *Self-managed learning*. A way of organising meta-learning together with colleagues.

This practical section of the book contains a selection from the many existing learning and working methods for learning groups. References are also included, however, in order to draw the reader's attention to other ways of learning with colleagues.

19
Peer consultation as a complement to education and practice

How does peer consultation fit in with Kolb's learning cycle?

Armed with the knowledge about learning and learning styles gained in Part III, we can take another look at the practice of peer consultation. Where exactly does peer consultation fit in within Kolb's learning styles? It has been suggested (e.g. in McGill and Beaty, 1992, or in Weinstein, 1995) that action learning stimulates the whole learning circle and stimulates every one of Kolb's learning styles equally. Our own research (see Appendix E for a summary) has shown a rather different situation, where action learning seems to stimulate one learning style – divergence – more than the others.[1] Peer consultation consists primarily of reflection and an exchange of ideas on the basis of (previous) experiences in work situations, and this means that peer consultation is set primarily within the divergent learning style.

The divergent learning style is present in all three roles within peer consultation.
1. *For the professional contributing an issue*, peer consultation means:
   – dwelling on a notable experience

1. Reg Revans, who coined the name 'action learning', seems to have been acutely aware of this:
   Every participant will, from time to time, find himself down another blind alley when he will discover for himself that there is little point in asking what his charismatic hero would have done ... if he is out of ideas, or needs to face mounting opposition on the job, the fellows will help him more clearly to perceive where he must look, for in doing so and in discussing why they are doing so, they will also be strengthening themselves. The mind gone blank can do little with itself save panic, but a few supportive minds aware that they themselves might, too, go blank at any moment can provide the most refreshing tonic. ... By needing to crawl along subterranean labyrinths, each fellow will come to respect the subtleties and the contradictions that compose his project; all these he will seek to balance and to record, constantly stopping and turning to ask what is still unseen. In this exploration he will put aside instant response and turn to considerate reflection (Revans, 1978, 2nd edn, p. 39).

- collecting questions, recommendations and potential solutions
- reflecting with others on the experience and the learning which may ensue from it.[1]

2. Learning *on the part of the consultants* in the consultation group is divergent because it centres on:
   - deferring judgment, and
   - asking questions as candidly and openly as possible.

   Consultants also learn in an accommodative manner, through the feedback they receive in response to their advice and consultancy behaviour. This is the case because they are indeed practising in a genuine consultancy situation and so improving their skills as consultants.

3. As far as the *facilitator of the consultation group* is concerned, Part II of this action guide deals with this area. The facilitator seems to be contributing mainly as a developer (see Chapter 16) who is strongly geared towards divergent learning by reflection and feedback on such aspects as:
   - the behaviour of both issue holder and consultants,
   - what is happening here-and-now in the consultation group
   - how the group can learn from difficult moments.

There are opportunities within peer consultation methods to apply a different learning style:

1. The clinic method is also concerned with accommodative learning of new behaviour, albeit not in the real situation with the real counter-parts but with the other members of the consultation group as stand-ins. The clinic method is therefore primarily a training method, which is used to 'train' new behaviour.

2. The dominant-ideas method sometimes crosses over the boundary to a more assimilative way of learning, when the discussion shifts towards the dominant world views or philosophies of the issue holder.

3. Another way of learning in a more assimilative manner occurs when the facilitator, responding to an event within the consultation group, adds some background information on a relevant subject (levels of intervention, group dynamics). This can also be the case in peer supervision (especially in the supervision method), where colleagues investigate a subject relevant to the profession (such as working procedures, jurisprudence, legislation or ICT systems) in greater depth.

In general, however, peer consultation is limited in terms of learning style.

1. Divergent *meta-learning* is therefore a common occurrence during peer consultation.

Interestingly, divergence is highly complementary to the learning styles which are common in most professions. Kolb (1984) summarises a variety of research into dominant learning styles, in different professions and positions within organisations. The results are roughly as follows:

1. *Divergent*: only a poor score for social workers and human resources.
2. *Assimilative*: a poor score for management; good scores for the research, development and finance departments.
3. *Convergent*: good scores for accountants, engineers and doctors, as well as the technical or technological departments.
4. *Accommodative*: good scores for teachers, career consultants, sports trainers, dieticians and the marketing department.

We can conclude from Kolb's research that most professionals have learned their fields mainly in the assimilative, convergent or accommodative learning styles. They are equipped with the subject matter necessary for their field (assimilation), have learned how to take decisions on the basis of that subject matter (convergence) and have learned to be active in their professional practice (accommodation). Precisely the divergent learning style that is central to the first two parts of this action guide is relatively absent from most professional training and is little addressed in day-to-day professional practice.

For an example from my own practice of the effects of peer consultation on leaders in a large organisation see Appendix F, which deals with a large-scale action learning initiative within the BBC.

What are the advantages of peer consultation?

• Peer consultation helps professionals to introduce a moment of *peace and quiet* into their sometimes extremely hectic practice. This peace and quiet, combined with the mutual support made possible by the open and safe learning climate, enables professionals to let questions and problems of which they were barely aware sink in and so devote more attention to them. They can also devote more attention to each other, and share each other's frustrations.

• Peer consultation invites professionals to *reflect together* and *slow down their thinking*, to defer judgment and conclusions. Professionals are often accustomed to reflecting about what they are doing (Schön, 1983), but those reflections remain individual and (largely) self-confirming. A major difference arises when they share their reflections with colleagues, after which they are inspired in turn by those colleagues' reflections. The links that develop in this way sometimes generate a degree of sensitivity and creativity, a new and surprising insight which is remarkable even to the professionals themselves. In particular, the treasure which can be unearthed by *connections*

Figure 19.1 'We are meditating today using the five-fold method'

between the issue raised and the situation here-and-now (see Chapter 11) is experienced in this respect as very productive in terms of insights.

- Peer consultation leads to deep *concentration* and a collective *focus* on the core issues. This makes it possible to achieve greater depth. It also makes it possible truly to invest in a question or problem – thanks to the methods, a problem can be held on to for longer than usual.
- Peer consultation is *complementary* to the ways in which professionals are accustomed to learning. Partly due to the creative nature of divergent learning, there is a high probability that this learning style really will add something new to help respond to the practical problems raised. Apart from that, the complementary nature of the learning style makes most professionals more 'rounded'- it enables them to develop further by means of all four learning styles and so, where necessary, to travel the full learning cycle. I notice in my practice that other complementary (divergent) learning activities such as coaching are also receiving increasing interest from professionals (see de Haan and Burger, 2004).

What are the drawbacks of learning in peer consultation groups?

Within peer consultation there is often too little attention paid to:

- *Application* in professionals' own practice: individuals' own practice remains outside the consultation group. The primarily *convergent* learning on the path towards application sometimes remains too detached.

- *Pressure* to bring about renewal and change – peer consultation is predominantly open and supportive, rather than judgmental, monitoring or supervisory. Pressure to change should therefore come from inside the issue holder him/herself. The primarily *accommodative* problem of actually putting into practice what has been learned sometimes remains underexposed.

- *Anchoring and structuring* what has been learned by means of theoretical models and previously developed knowledge – this is confined to what happens to be contributed to the relevant consultation group. The solutions to a question thus remain confined to what the participants can come up with themselves. Moreover, by talking and thinking about specific experiences and instruments, we are not encouraging the link between what has been learned and more general literature and knowledge. This, of course, is not an optimal, 'scientifically well-founded' procedure for achieving objective improvement. The primarily *assimilative* style of learning from the more theoretical fruits of the experiences and reflections of experienced professionals therefore comes into play in peer consultation only if those more experienced professionals are themselves present and opt to make a theoretical contribution.

However, let us not forget that peer consultation, despite these disadvantages,[1] has a major strength as a learning activity – it is by visiting and revisiting this

---

1. Besides the research described in Appendix E, there is Maarten Driehuis' thesis (1997), a quantitative study conducted in action learning groups of independent management consultants. Driehuis points out further disadvantages, from a more strategic and long-term perspective. In his view, it is difficult to achieve sufficient depth within peer consultation. Many action learning groups appear to have difficulty actually putting into practice the suggestions about asking questions and mutual learning presented in the first parts of this action guide. The results of Driehuis' research can be summarised as follows:
    1. *Results of action learning*:
       a. (positive) critical reflection and new understanding of one's own professional actions
       b. (positive) incentive to direct one's own actions
       c. (positive) learning situation experienced as enjoyable and worthwhile
       d. (negative) little understanding of underlying factors ('hidden operators') which influence one's own actions
       e. (negative) little application in the form of long-term effect on own actions.

cont. over

particular reflective learning style that most true professionals, be they managers or consultants, keep their learning edge.

Conclusion

Looking at peer consultation through Kolb's eyes, it is noticeable that supervision and action learning rely primarily on divergent learning styles. For most professionals, this is a complementary way of learning compared with their own training or with learning through experience in their own professional practice. An exception to this is the learning of the consultants themselves, who develop their consultation skills both in their work and in the role of consultant within peer consultation. This marked emphasis on the divergent learning style can be seen as a great strength and depth of peer consultation, but it can also be viewed as a disadvantage, as a restriction on learning with colleagues.

However, it is eminently possible, and often useful, to go beyond peer consultation by means of learning activities which come 'closer to the work' than peer consultation and action learning with colleagues. Then, successes and results within the professionals' own practice will be associated more closely with personal development. This calls for a greater willingness to learn from their own mistakes and uncertainties from the participants. If that willingness is there, a range of techniques and methods discussed so far under the heading of 'peer consultation' can also be applied within the professionals' own work (project-based action learning, see Chapter 21) or in devising and planning learning activities (learning networks, see Chapter 22).

An example: Erik's diary of *Learning with Colleagues* (5)

14 December 1999: a new incentive
In a department of a ministry, management and staff determine that they are working in too much isolation and not learning enough from each other. The new head of the department wants to devote more attention to learning from one's own and each other's work. We are asked to support the creation and introduction of peer consultation in a variety of

2. *Causes of disappointing results*:
   a. Personal 'standards' are not explicit enough, resulting in too little internal pressure on learning results.
   b. Too 'liberal' an environment, resulting in too little group pressure on learning results.
   c. Too little correspondence with own professional context with a view to long-term results. Lack of orientation towards integrating learning results into the professional's own practice. Following on from this, Driehuis recommends improving the quality of action learning by means of a better connection with, and anchoring in, the consultant's own work. Moreover, he gives a range of suggestions relating to a more strategic use of the instrument.

forms. The intention is that some staff and managers from the department itself should learn to facilitate various consultation activities. The ministry wants to use our texts and, what is more, devote a page to peer consultation on its own intranet. A good reason to take another look at the written material produced by my colleagues, and re-compile it for the learning process with the colleagues from the ministry.

In this project I am working with Ina, a new colleague. Ina certainly knows a lot about learning as a teacher and trainer, but she hasn't facilitated peer consultation groups in this form before. Partly in order to show her the ropes, it appears to be useful to have a clear summary of the consultation methods on paper.

I am working on a 'Peer consultation workbook' in two parts. To that end I am using the texts produced by Adrie and Heleen, which I am revising and supplementing with new methods and a more detailed text on learning from connections between there-and-then and here-and-now. We are giving the two parts to this client, but we are also bringing them to the attention of other colleagues.

A complement to education and practice

The current writing activities are clearly complementary to my practice, which was heavily focused on facilitating learning with colleagues. After a fairly long period during which I was focused in a practical sense on helping learning groups to get started, it is a relief to be writing about this subject again. It helps that both this new client and this relatively new colleague are proving very helpful in requesting clear texts on this subject. There is therefore a clear demand for the work that I am currently doing. I am not learning very much myself at this time; instead, I am more concerned with helping my client and colleague to get started in a different way, namely by redrafting the existing reader.

Summary: peer consultation as a complement to education and practice

Peer consultation consists of mutual learning, where in any case the learning on the part of the issue holder is primarily *divergent*.

Divergent learning can be shown to arise in:

- dwelling on a notable experience
- a joint search for problems, advice and potential solutions
- reflection on the experience, and on the learning which may ensue from it
- the facilitators' style of working – primarily facilitating in a developing way.

Advantages of learning within peer consultation

- the *peace and quiet* to distance oneself from a sometimes hectic professional practice
- the supportive nature of the consultation group, and the open and *safe learning climate*
- the *sharing* of frustrations about, and reflections on, problematic situations
- learning from the *reflections* of there-and-then in the here-and-now.
- the deep *concentration* that is possible in the consultation group
- the *focus* that arises from taking time to think without judging and without pressure to make decisions
- the reflective *depth* that can be achieved in the consultation group
- a learning style that is *complementary* to that of many training methods for professionals, and of too much on-the-job learning.

Drawbacks of learning in peer consultation groups

- *application* in professionals' own practice
- *external pressure* to bring about renewal and change
- *critical examination* of what is achieved in the consultation group
- *anchoring and structuring* what has been learned by means of theoretical concepts and previously developed knowledge.

20
Extension I:
Short-cycle learning

Learning on the basis of the full Kolb model is quite possible. It can take place, for example, in the form of the EQCS model. This instrument is very useful if you have to 'improvise' something on a given subject in a training course or conference, for example at the participants' request. If you, as the facilitator, are well-versed in the subject matter you can use this instrument to design, within the space of ten minutes, a morning or afternoon during which the subject can be discussed thoroughly from every angle. The abbreviation EQCS makes the method easier to remember. This is useful because the method is applicable primarily to unforeseen circumstances. The EQCS model is set out in Figure 20.1.

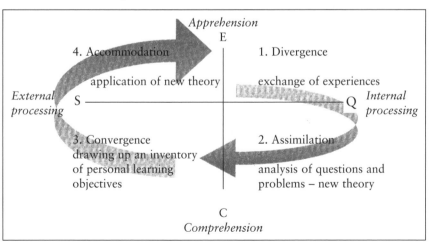

Figure 20.1 *The EQCS model*

E Experiences

Start at the top of the diagram with the specific experience. Make a link to the experiences of the participants. Ask them about their experiences; ask how they came across this subject in their work, for example, and what they have learned about it previously. Tell them something of your own experience of the subject, perhaps in the form of an anecdote, and say what you found most instructive.

Q Questions

Now move on to the questions surrounding this subject. If the subject relates to a request from the participants, there will be a specific reason which can be put into words as a question or problem. Link as far as possible to problems or questions familiar to the participants or (preferably) which they have encountered themselves previously.

Organise a joint reflection on these questions and problems. Try to reach a deeper level where, for example:

- different questions can be connected with each other, or
- patterns are recognised within and between the questions.

C Concepts

Only now do you, as facilitator, say something about the content of the chosen subject. Only now is it appropriate to introduce information, models and theories. The advantage is that this knowledge follows on almost automatically from problems experienced by participants, questions which they have or reflections being undertaken jointly at this time. If it doesn't, then it will be clear, from the vantage point of your expertise and knowledge, that they have been asking the wrong questions.

S Skills

Don't forget to pay attention to the application of new knowledge. This application is best done in two stages (convergent and accommodative):

- First draw up a list of personal learning goals or identify parts of the theory that participants want to apply.
- Then apply the aspects identified to a situation, case or exercise which is as realistic as possible, or even to the work practice itself (see also the next chapter, on project-based action learning).

E This experience

At the end of the learning experience, all participants look back together at the original requests for learning, outstanding learning questions and the usefulness of this experience. By reflecting on the effects of the EQCS model, they sometimes arrive automatically at meta-learning on the chosen subject (as may be evidenced by reflections such as 'I should have read more about it', or 'You see that you simply need the nerve to try new things').

An example

We thought it worthwhile to do something on the subject of learning at the start of the first three-day module of a ten-day project management course. We knew that the participants varied widely in terms of experience – they included novice project managers but also experienced project leaders who regularly completed major projects successfully in difficult, political contexts.

(*Divergent*) We start that morning with the question: 'How have you learned about project management in projects and courses so far?' We write the answers to this question under the heading E on the flip-chart. The answers from this group are very diverse, as expected.

We then establish, together with the participants, that we are dealing with a wide diversity of backgrounds and experiences. We write 'diversity' on the flip-chart under the heading Q. We admit that it is a challenge for us to develop a project management course with them under these conditions. We stress that it is important for us that they should also learn a lot from each other during the course. At that point we notice the first signs of curiosity in the group about the meaning of the letters E and Q.

We put the following question to the group: 'How do we tackle this?', and conclude provisionally that it is advisable to work with a programme which is as varied as possible and with a lot of mutual, personal feedback.

(*Assimilative*) Now we take the learning style inventory (see Appendix D) and ask each project manager to fill in a copy. Meanwhile, we draw a heading B on the flip-chart. We also prepare coloured boards headed E, Q, C and S, which we attach to the four walls of the room. After completing the inventory, we present our introduction to learning and Kolb's learning styles. In the group as a whole, we draw up a list of the preferred styles within the group and ask if participants are able to recognise themselves in the scores which they have calculated for themselves.

NB: it is often striking how well participants recognise the results of this inventory, even though it consists only of 12 simple questions, in their own learning activities. Only the 'assimilators' sometimes challenge those results, but this phenomenon in itself may be taken as confirmation of their assimilative learning style.

(*Convergent*) We ask participants to choose one clear preferred style for themselves, so as to choose their strongest learning style. Then we ask them to connect two of the main learning objectives which they have in this programme to the four learning styles, in order to find the most appropriate learning style for each of those two questions. At this point there is some discussion, partly because their own personal learning styles and the connection between learning objectives and learning styles are still unclear. By steering the discussion and helping participants to choose, we are able to complete this section successfully.

(*Accommodative*) Then we write an S on the flip-chart and ask the participants, on the basis of their preferred style, to go to one of the four corners of the room. They therefore have to stand between the letters E and Q, or between Q and C, or between C and S, or between S and E, whichever corresponds best to their personal learning style. The learning styles are ultimately between these pairs of letters.

In these subgroups of 'similarly learning participants', we ask them to complete the following sentence: 'What I have learned in the past as a project manager with this learning style ...' In the final part of the morning, they must actively seek support (in the form of feedback, reflections, suggested literature, and so on) from the other groups for the two learning questions which they earlier classified as belonging to a specific style.

(*Divergent*) Just before lunch, we write the letter E on the chart and take a look back, as a group, at this morning's learning activities. How do the participants experience this session (E)? How do they now view the questions which they had at the start of the morning (Q)? Did Kolb's model come across at all (C)? Have they gained more skill in applying the learning styles as a result of their activities (S)?

This book *Learning with Colleagues* as an example of the EQCS model

As has already been pointed out in the preface, this entire action guide is organised as an 'EQCS model' – at least insofar as any book which in itself is oriented inwards, and so promotes mainly divergence and assimilation, can cover all of the learning styles. I start in Part I by getting to the point as quickly as possible and encouraging consultation groups to gain experiences (E); then Parts I and II contain a number of chapters which help to learn from questions arising in consultation groups (Q); Part III mainly contains information from theory (C); Part IV concludes with a number of chapters aimed at helping learning groups choose between different learning forms and to develop optimal activities with a view to learning (S).

Application to peer supervision and action learning

Consultation group members who mainly discuss questions and problems (Q) with each other (hence emphasising divergence) during the sessions can arrange to return in the next session to an issue raised in the current one. Prior to a new contribution they discuss:

E: new experiences which the previous session's issue holder has had, thanks to the reflections in the consultation group

C: any new concepts or literature which the issue holder has studied

S: what action the issue holder has taken in practice on the basis of what was learned in the previous session.

In this way, they can extend the work done in the consultation group and make a closer connection with their professional practice in the intervals between sessions. It is worth noting that:

- This approach requires greater discipline, both from the issue holder in the consultation group and from the other participants.
- There is a risk that an action learning group will become too critical and supervisory as a result, and that participants will be more reluctant to raise issues because they know they will be challenged to 'do something' in practice.

It may be advisable to agree explicitly in an action learning group that the issue holder does not need to view the conclusions as homework for his or her own practice!

Figure 20.2 *Short-cycle learning: learning under pressure*

An example: Erik's diary of *Learning with Colleagues* (6)

7 June 2000: everything is falling into place

The two parts of the 'Peer consultation workbook' appear to be catching on with colleagues. Virtually everyone involved in the facilitation of consultation groups is using Part I, and in many cases my colleagues are also using Part II, to help develop facilitators of action learning groups. These colleagues are also commenting usefully on the texts and asking for illustrations and diagrams. This encourages me to rewrite Part II again and ask Selma van Vemde to prepare some illustrations.

But I am also submerging myself in the old literature again, reading James, Jung, Dewey, Lewin, Piaget and others with renewed interest. Now I am reading Kolb too, the author who is cited so frequently when it comes to learning. His book is a revelation. Kolb writes clearly and methodically about various learning styles and backs up his examples with results from his own research. In addition, he is honest about his debt to many other authors who developed cyclical learning models independently of each other. This Kolb seems totally different in a number of respects from the Kolb I had heard so much about. The travelling of the full learning cycle, for example, which is often seen as characteristic of learning, seems to be completely unnecessary for Kolb. According to him, you can also stay in one learning style, where you can learn what you have to learn. I agree with him entirely and now decide to write a third section of the action guide about learning itself, based to a large extent on Kolb.

Short-cycle learning

After the success of the 'workbook' with both client and colleagues, I am travelling Kolb's full learning cycle in miniature – the positive experiences lead directly to reflection on how things could be even better, which leads to my plunging again into the literature. After reading Kolb I am thinking about the EQCS model again, the method I learned over six years ago from freelance trainer Peter Siebrands. I am now going to apply that method again, as in the example in Chapter 20. These experiences, taken together, are giving a new impetus to my practice as a 'learning facilitator' – I am going to broaden my approach and put things like short-cycle learning and project-based action learning into practice more frequently. Which of course leads in turn to new experiences from which I can learn.

Summary: short-cycle learning

The EQCS model is an easy-to-remember instrument, which can be used to facilitate learning quickly and comprehensively with a group of participants and some requested subject matter.

Instructions for facilitators of the EQCS model:
E   *Experiences*: Start with the specific experience of participants and ask questions on that basis.
Q   *Questions*: Investigate which questions and problems come to the fore in the experience and think about them.
C   *Concepts*: Now tell the group something of your own expertise and knowledge in relation to the subject and apply those to participants' experiences and problems.
S   *Skills*: Make sure that participants actually get down to work with the new knowledge, in an exercise or practical assignment.
E   *Experience*: Take a look back together at the session and its usefulness.

The structure of the EQCS model can also be used to broaden learning within consultation groups. This requires extra discipline, and attention to the fact that the quality of the consultation itself may deteriorate as a result.

21
Extension II:
Project-based action learning

Project-based action learning is a way of setting up peer consultation in existing teams, such as project groups or management teams. The team members become 'comrades in adversity' (Revans, 1978), who help each other through a common project and learn from it as it unfolds, while they feed the learning back into the project itself and their professional practice (Casey, 1976).

Because of this dual stress on managing the project and drawing out the learning, this chapter focuses on efforts to address opposite learning styles in Kolb's model at the same time, or to learn in both polarities simultaneously.

What is project-based action learning?

Mixing opposite learning styles can be a very elaborate and tense process. When you mix opposite learning styles, you bring disparate worlds together – worlds that do not observe the same standards, and where units and meaning are completely different, so that they cannot be understood using a shared language. The mixing of opposite learning styles can result in ambiguous communication, which may, for example, be ironic (see de Haan, 1999) or paradoxical (see Watzlawick, Beavin and Jackson, 1967). This ambiguous, internally contradictory communication can be very conducive to learning, in my view, because of the creative tension generated.

Two terms can be used to describe these interesting mixes (Figures 21.1 and 21.2).
1. *Reflection in action.* Reflection in action is a learning method in which learners experiment with new actions and think about them at the same time. Sometimes, reflection in action arises when experts explain what they are doing while they are doing it, or when pupils at school learn while thinking aloud (e.g. Schön, 1983). Another method is reflection on what is happening here-and-now (see Chapter 11) – in the here-and-now

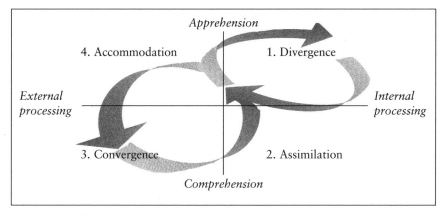

Figure 21.1 *Project-based action learning: reflection in action*

each communicative act is an action, so when someone thinks about that act itself, reflection in action results immediately. This is why here-and-now interventions are so powerful. Reflection in action is primarily an attempt to mix divergence and convergence.

2. *Congruent modelling.* Congruent modelling is a learning strategy in which learners allow 'living' and 'teaching' to reinforce each other. They choose learning and working methods where they neither adapt nor subordinate the complex reality to the model, nor subordinate the model to action by applying only one element or derivation. Using congruent modelling, learners quite literally 'practise what they preach'. They transpose the model fully into action or take the result of the action as a model. In so doing, they achieve maximum congruence between form and content – in other words, between the approach to learning and

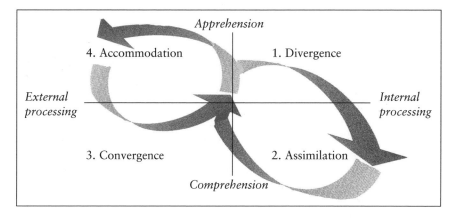

Figure 21.2 *Project-based action learning: congruent modelling*

what is learned. Congruent modelling is therefore primarily an attempt to mix assimilation and accommodation.

According to Reg Revans, the founding father of project-based action learning, the history of this concept dates back to the *Titanic* disaster in 1912 (Marquardt, 1999). Revans' father was one of those who investigated the claim after the disaster. What he discovered was that many planners and builders had been afraid beforehand that the ship was not soundly enough constructed, but most of them had remained silent on the assumption that everything would be fine if no one else mentioned it. Intrigued, in the 1930s Reg Revans began to develop techniques to bring learning and working so close together that the results would be more reliable. Project-based action learning is therefore as much a working and developing method as a learning method.

The main principles of project-based action learning[1]

Learning and working should lie as close together as possible. The project-based action learning group works on a problem or project which has considerable relevance and urgency for its own work. The problem must not have a known solution – in other words, the solution must not already have been found by others. Indeed, the problem usually does not have any unique or 'best' solution. Responsibility for the project lies entirely with the project-based action learning group. It is not usual to appoint a (project) leader within the group because this would jeopardise the equal responsibility held by all members for both actions and learning.

A sponsor is needed for project-based action learning, but this role is lighter than that of the client in a project. This is because the group members in project-based action learning are the problem holders themselves, so they are themselves the parties most interested in bringing the project to a successful conclusion. The sponsor's duties include only concern for connections with the rest of the organisation and making available the necessary time and resources.

Peer consultation is central. Learning and working take place in a group of (preferably) four to eight participants. Colleagues who work together frequently meet in order to bring the project to a successful conclusion. Because eligible problem holders and specialists are members of the group, the project-based action learning method assumes that learning takes place primarily within the group and that it will not be necessary to bring in external knowledge and facts – 'Use the project as a textbook and the colleague as a teacher' (Revans, 1978). The learning

1. Marquardt (1999) mentions six 'components' of project-based action learning: the problem, the group, asking questions and reflecting, resolution to proceed to action, commitment to learning, and the facilitator.

and working colleagues interpret their own problems and questions themselves, and so generate solutions themselves. As in peer consultation, the inwards oriented learning is therefore primarily divergent, and less assimilative.

In project-based action learning groups, participants take time explicitly to reflect, and try to arrive at an action plan after each joint reflection. This means that 'divergence' and 'convergence' can follow each other in the group. 'There is no real learning unless action is taken' (Marquardt, 1999).

There is always a facilitator present, who focuses on the progress of learning and working. The facilitator's role is not easy because (s)he must facilitate all four learning styles if necessary. It is advisable to allocate this role to colleagues with experience in previous action learning projects, or to work with an external facilitator.

Project-based action learning, like peer consultation, works with three roles during the session – an issue holder (who changes from session to session), the other participants and the facilitator. Sometimes the role of issue holder will be taken by more than one participant, or even by the whole group.

Figure 21.3 *Action learning at work*

Salient differences between project-based action learning and peer consultation

- Extending of learning behaviour over all four of Kolb's learning styles.
- Regular work is not interrupted but carries on as usual within the project-based action learning. It is necessary, however, to allow more time than usual for reflection and questioning.
- Colleagues usually come from the same organisation and are problem holders together.
- The facilitator's role is completely different. As well as being a developer, the facilitator must also be a process manager, organiser and sometimes even an expert (compare Chapter 16). In addition, assuming the role of developer involves further difficulty – it is hard to lead the group to a divergent style (observing, listening, asking questions, deferring judgment, and so on) in the middle of a turbulent and exciting project.[1] Experience has shown that it is particularly difficult to get the accommodators (or 'activists') to learn. It is often necessary to work at a higher frequency in project-based action learning than in consultation. Meeting once every six to eight weeks is often not enough, given the urgency which should be associated with project-based action learning projects.

A project-based action learning session takes up a good morning or afternoon, and the agenda may look something like this:

1. *Opening*: Review of present state of affairs, current topics and most pressing problems.
2. *Reflection on past actions*: A peer consultation approach intended to clarify the problem and think about it together. Almost every supervision or action learning method is eligible, although the methods which focus more to the person of the issue holder (dominant-ideas method, gossip method, clinic method) are often less suitable here. Methods eminently applicable to project-based action learning are the learn-and-explore method and learning from success. The U-method can also be used, with the sole drawback that it is rather hypothetical in nature ('What if …?') and so less geared towards action.

---

1. In an interesting piece of research, Jennings (2002) confirms that it is very difficult to make project-based action learning work. In the context of strategic management programmes in a business school, three very interactive and practical learning methods are compared – case study, business simulation, and project-based action learning. Project-based action learning emerges as the least successful of the three, with respect to most of the criteria studied (such as knowledge transfer, problem solving, self-awareness, collaboration, behaviour change, management perspective, adding realism to the course). Jennings mentions (1) the strenuous relationships with other managers and with organisational politics, (2) the time commitment required, and (3) lack of control over the learning situation, as causes for dissatisfaction with this type of action learning.

3. *Reflection on future actions*: Before subsequent actions are planned, the group members think together about priorities, desired results, risks, and so on.

4 *Reflection on the group itself* (here-and-now reflection in action):
   - What is the level of commitment, involvement, progress, etc.?
   - Who takes what action until the next session (planning)?
   - What does the group feel about the climate of, and the relationships within, this project-based action learning group?

5. *Winding up*: What else is on the table?

If this works well, the entire session is a moment of reflection in action. If the action learning group arrives at solutions which have to be implemented, they can think through this implementation and even simulate it within the session. For project-based action learning to succeed, it is essential that learning and working should stay as close together as possible, and that whatever reaches one pole should reach the other as well.

The project-based action learning group therefore works diagonally and in all four learning styles as far as possible:

- Results of divergence should be converted into a decision or plan as quickly as possible.
- Results of assimilation should be realised as actions.
- Results of convergence should find form in new reflections.
- Results of accommodation should feed into new models.

In my view, this makes project-based action learning, with its rapid alternation both between thinking and applying (reflection in action) and analysing and doing (congruent modelling), the best approach to uniting the polarities. A true union of the opposite polarities is not possible. At best, there will be a tense and uneasy compromise which is capable of maintaining a fragile connection between learning and working.

An example: Erik's diary of *Learning with Colleagues* (7)

8 September 2000: painful feedback
Now that the summer is over the third and fourth parts are ready, with various models but also some practical additions concerning peer consultation, which I present as 'extensions'. Again, I ask a selection of colleagues to read this new text. Now their reaction is less positive, however. Except from a couple of colleagues who have long been enthusiastic about David Kolb's learning styles, Part III meets with opposition. Some colleagues find the text needlessly dull and complicated. In their view, this section does not give a complete picture of learning and learning groups.

This feedback has two important consequences for me. First, I feel for the first time that I myself am really 'behind' this text, and therefore can take the risk of being stubborn. Second, I decide to do something with the many diary entries I have collected. I want to use them to lighten Parts III and IV with some of my own 'learning in practice'.

Project-based action learning

The first version of Part IV was written in the summer of 2000, at some distance from my professional practice which, as usual, is a bit quieter in the summer than in the rest of the year. During this period I bury myself in a pile of books and, as I study, work out a story that runs from peer consultation to project learning groups and learning networks. For quite a while I do not show my writing to colleagues, nor do I experiment myself with what I am writing. When I do contact colleagues and clients again, I find I have estranged myself from them somewhat with my texts, as they are not really able to follow what I have done.

It is painful for me to hear their comments after many hours of intensive writing. I am reminded that it is better for me to link learning to action more closely and to review it more frequently in my own practice.

Summary: project-based action learning

Project-based action learning is a learning and working method directed towards the development of products/services, colleagues, and the organisation (at the same time!).

An essential aspect of project-based action learning is that learning and working are brought as close together as possible, so that opposite learning styles in Kolb's model are, as far as possible, addressed simultaneously or in quick succession:

- When learning has occurred, the question is: What is the accompanying action?
- When actions have taken place: What can we learn from them?
- *Reflection in action*: Bringing together divergent and convergent learning.
- *Congruent modelling*: Bringing together assimilative and accommodative learning.

Principles of project-based action learning
- Within a project with considerable relevance and urgency for group members.
- With a sponsor who, working in the background, takes care of connections and resources.
- In a learning group of problem holders and specialists, without a project manager.
- Emphasis on reflection and action planning during the sessions.
- With a facilitator for the project-based action learning group.

How does project-based action learning differ from peer consultation?
- Broadening out to make use of other learning styles.
- Regular work fits in with the learning group, and colleagues are often problem-holders together.
- A facilitator of project-based action learning groups has a broader responsibility than a facilitator of consultation groups.
- Greater frequency of sessions, inspired by the ongoing project.

22
Extension III: Self-managed learning and learning networks

Every time we learn something, we are undertaking a learning activity and at the same time gaining experience of learning itself. Meta-learning is therefore always an issue. Bateson (1942), perhaps the first person to draw attention to this fact, called learning about learning 'deuterolearning'. In this chapter, this second-order learning activity is broadened out into a final extension of peer consultation – self-managed learning.

It has been demonstrated for many learning activities that the quality of meta-learning in particular is critical for the efficiency and effectiveness of the learning process. It is therefore worthwhile taking a look at learning activities which address meta-learning in particular.

Before we do so, I would like to point out once again that I do not advocate a self-managed approach in every learning situation. In my view, self-managed learning also has major disadvantages:

- Extensive freedom and autonomy can sometimes turn against the learner.
- Motivational problems may arise.
- Emphasis on self-management may mean that learners have less time for the learning itself, due to all of the 'meta-work'.
- A high degree of self-management means that learners are less compliant, so they may – in sublime ignorance – disregard good advice from instructors.

Despite these reservations, I remain very enthusiastic about self-managed learning provided it is applied to the right questions. For example, it may be appropriate for questions from groups that:

- have already learned a lot within different learning activities, such as peer consultation, and
- have achieved a high degree of independence and motivation for action learning.

In other words, groups whose enthusiasm makes them a pleasure to work with! I frequently err in my own assessment of whether a self-managed approach is appropriate. I notice that choosing self-managed learning in a situation where participants are not ready for it often leads to confusion, and sometimes even to conflict between facilitators and participants. Such situations are difficult to turn around to a positive climate for learning. At the same time, continuing commitment by participants in a confusing situation is a sign that self-managed learning is possible, though not always easy ...

An example

At the start of a lecture cycle for graduate students, I ask the question which always comes up in self-managed learning: "What do you actually want to learn from me?" This question immediately generates confusion. Doesn't the lecturer decide what is on the curriculum? Can't he just tell us 'something' from his own practice? Or perhaps 'discuss' the set literature?

In the next lecture we make a second attempt – an à la carte menu. On the menu, which contains diverse topics and working methods, the time needed is now stated beside each item. The total time needed is sufficient for three lectures. More confusion. All of this looks very interesting, say the students. Can't we do all of it? – and, perhaps, shorten each subject a bit? Can't the lecturer tell us what is 'most interesting' and discuss that?

It is clear that the students are not yet accustomed to self-managed learning ...

We try again in subsequent lectures, by having students draw up their own lists of learning questions, by asking them to contribute their own cases and by making time on each occasion to consider what should be on the agenda. However, in spite of – or perhaps because of – the students' compliant and flexible responses, the situation never really develops into one where they are managing the learning process themselves.

At the end of the cycle we carry out a written evaluation. The students seem to have found the lectures interesting and 'out of the ordinary' but their main impression is that the same subject matter could have been conveyed much more quickly ... why spend so much time talking about what should be on the agenda ...?!![1]

What is self-managed learning?

Self-managed learning consists of three components, which recur in the literature under different names (see for example Corno, 1986). The first two correspond to the 'inward processing' and 'outward processing' poles in Kolb's model (1984):

1. In his article on self-managed learning, Rogers (1957) gives an example in which he went even further, leaving the initiative for all activity and for the 'use' of the teacher entirely to the students. The confusion he reports in his group is proportionate – i.e. considerably greater than in my example!

1. *Self-monitoring*: Looking in a detached, critical manner at how you learn. Checking whether this way of learning is effective; gathering information about your own way of learning, in relation to alternative ways of learning.
2. *Self-direction*: Taking action in order to use the information you have gathered about your own learning, so as to direct yourself in the way you learn best; selecting learning behaviour appropriate to the situation; experimenting with alternative learning behaviour.
3. *Self-motivation*: Being able to motivate yourself when necessary; developing perseverance; being able to judge a learning activity in terms of future results.

Other terms are often used in connection with self-management: autonomy, personal responsibility and affective regulation among others.

There is something paradoxical about creating 'self-management' from the outside, because the message given is then: 'Direct yourself, upon my orders!'. There is some entertaining literature about attempts by external consultants to create 'self-managed learning situations'. Roger Harrison's autobiography (1995) and 'Personal thoughts on teaching and learning' by Carl Rogers (1957) are worth reading in this respect. This literature describes struggles at many points, both within the learners and the learning consultant.

The knack appears to be to tackle these struggles head on and convert them into results, preventing the learning activity from going under in the struggle. Harrison introduces a metaphor with a flavour of the Middle Ages, that of the 'castle' and 'battlefield' (Harrison, 1963). According to him, both are necessary for self-managed learning:

- the castle as the safe stronghold to which we can retreat, the base from which we can accept uncertainties
- the battlefield as the place where we come to the painful realisation that we still have something to learn, and that it is hard to learn; the place where we let go of certainties and try out something new.

What is needed to establish self-managed learning with colleagues?

Below are a number of suggestions from my experience of working with learning groups. They are based on situations where an external facilitator or 'learning consultant' is present to facilitate the learning. However, an external consultant is often unnecessary during self-managed learning (Figure 22.1).

1. *Sufficient external structure* in order to be able to cope with as much freedom as possible internally (in the metaphor referred to above – a strong 'castle' outside, in order to make a 'battlefield' possible inside). The following are helpful in this respect:

- clarity about the expected or required learning results (from clients or managers)
- structure in the planning of sessions (fixed working hours, fixed frequency)
- structure in the planning of personal development (such as personal development plans, personal learning contracts, or a 'learning log')
- structure in the contribution made by the learning consultant. The latter presents him/herself as an expert in the field of learning, and if appropriate also in the subject matter, and makes it clear what can and cannot be learned from him or her.

2. *Sufficient external fuelling of the learning process*:
- Participants actively seek out new concepts, experts and experiences to enable them to develop further.
- On request, the learning consultant conveys knowledge to fuel the group.
- The learning consultant supports and helps the participants where possible – by honest evaluation and involvement, (s)he can help to ease the struggle of self-managed learning.

3. *'Hands-off' by all external parties*:
- Clients and managers leave the learning group free in its choice of learning activities and the formulation of results.

Figure 22.1 *In self-managed learning, the facilitator becomes superfluous*

- The learning consultant takes as little of the initiative as possible, makes no choices, gives no advice or direction, but adopts an anticipating and facilitating stance. This role is more detached than that set out in Part II for the facilitators of peer consultation groups.
4. *As much freedom of choice as possible*:
   - Managers and other interested parties refrain from making choices – they pass choices and decisions back to the participants as much as possible.
   - If a detached stance is not working, the learning consultant offers as wide as possible a range of content and working methods, preferably all attractive ones.
   - If a learning group or a participant has made a certain choice, the consultant will view the choice critically. Why choose this and not something else? And does the person concerned really know for sure?

Learning networks as an example of self-managed learning

Self-managed learning can be designed in a variety of ways. What is essential is that it should be designed by the participants themselves. Self-managed learning is ideal for individual learning.

As an illustration of an application of self-managed learning in learning groups, we discuss 'learning networks' here (see van der Krogt, 1998). Cunningham (1994) discusses another interesting approach to self-managed learning.

The main principles of learning networks

- The network is contracted between four to ten colleagues, to extend over a period of at least a year.
- As in peer consultation, the participants may include colleagues from the same organisation and professionals from different organisations.
- Participants manage the learning required for their work themselves. Within the network participants discuss learning activities, motivation and ambition.
- Participants link their activities with organisational objectives and with participants' long-term learning objectives. Learning activities take place as close as possible to the learner's own place of work. The express intention in the learning network is to learn from each others' expertise and from each others' approach in the field of management.
- Participants also contract with their managers and staff. A learning network organises training activities autonomously and often has its own budget. The organisation of such activities is traditionally the domain of senior management, which often delegates it to staff consultants in the field of human resources or management training. It is therefore a good idea to ask these managers frequently what, in their view, the network

should learn, and to have them seek advice from staff departments. The tension between 'what management decides' and 'what participants devise themselves' is productive when it comes to learning: participants assume greater personal responsibility than if they were to undertake learning activities only at the request of management or staff.

- Participants devise, plan, organise and implement learning activities. This gives rise to three activities in the learning network (van der Krogt, 1998):

  1. Charting a course along which the learning network can develop – this results in training plans and personal development plans, from management and participants respectively.
  2. Programming learning courses and programme components – in consultation with specialists in this field.
  3. Working through programmed learning courses – either as a learning network or in a different context.

Salient differences between self-managed learning and peer consultation or project-based action learning

- Extension of learning behaviour to the planning, organisation and management of the learning itself.
- Many of the more traditional learning activities of, and between, colleagues (such as consultation, training, literature study, and so on) now take place outside the network but – both in terms of subject-matter and physically – as close as possible to the place of work. Participants organise these learning activities for those who need them. The activities are sometimes individual, sometimes for larger groups and departments.
- The facilitator's role is completely different. The facilitator (if any!) is present only at the request of the learning network, and makes a contribution only after a direct request to do so. The facilitator is expected to provide expertise primarily with regard to learning itself.
- Considerable discipline and dedication is necessary to maintain the learning network and ensure that it is productive. Permanent commitment from senior management and regular evaluation with an external facilitator help to keep the learning network alive.

By way of a summary, there follow three illustrations to highlight the differences between peer consultation, project-based action learning and learning networks. The illustrations show a considerable simplification of what really happens in organisations. Only three processes are distinguished:

- *Working*, which includes not only the primary process of the organisation, but also a whole range of jobs and tasks that employees take on for various reasons.

- *Managing* (or control), which includes not only the management of the organisation, but also a range of local management tasks such as the development of a departmental strategy, annual departmental plans, a planning and control cycle, meetings, and so on.
- *Learning*, in other words all efforts to acquire knowledge in order to bring about improvements in the other two processes.

Each of these three processes is given its own symbol (Figure 22.2).

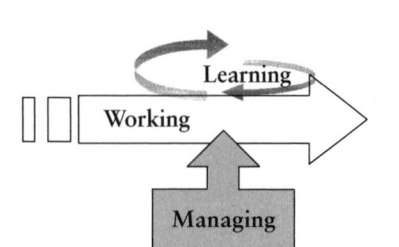

A: *Learning separate from working.* This is found in peer consultation but also in other familiar learning methods such as training or coaching. Separating learning from the workplace has pros and cons. It is easier to create an optimum working environment on the one hand but, on the other hand, all sorts of 'transfer problems' can arise in relation to bringing what has been learned into the workplace.

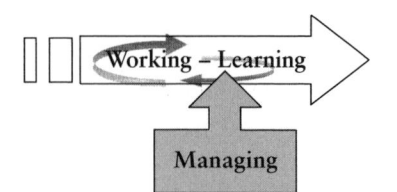

B: *Learning integrated with working.* This is the objective of project-based action learning.

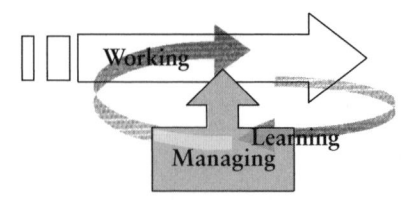

C: *Meta-learning integrated with working.* The situation envisaged in self-managed learning and learning networks

Figure 22.2 *Learning and working*

An example: Erik's diary of *Learning with Colleagues* (8)

18 October 2000: you can never learn enough

Today Ina tells me again about Argyris and Schön and their 'reflective practice' (Schön, 1987). Unfortunately, in recent weeks an unwelcome pattern has developed between Ina and myself when we talk about these theories. Ina talks enthusiastically and with inspiration and I listen patiently but conclude with the criticism: 'But isn't that just old wine in new bottles?' This time it is different. Finally I realise that here, in the comparison of 'espoused theory' and 'theory in use', something special is actually happening, and that this 'left-column' method can be used to invite people to take a fresh look at their own assumptions.

Too late, I realise that my Part III on learning was one-sided in its marked emphasis on Kolb. More people are coming up to me with other interesting books about learning which I have never heard of. What now? Does the writing process enter a new phase? Do I have to work on a new section?

I decide to leave the book as it is. Together with Adrie, Ina and six other colleagues, however, I decide to initiate a new learning network entitled 'The art of learning'. This will undoubtedly yield more new prospects and new learning experiences with colleagues.

Self-managed learning

What have I actually learned from writing this book? If I look back at the eight diary extracts which describe the process of creating this book, I notice that it has been more about learning than about teaching. Although the whole adventure started with a lack of direction, with no more than a few clumsy attempts to teach, I quickly began to learn from the search for a collaborative relationship, and from our doubts about it. In the period when I was not working on the book, I learned a lot in my practice in particular, and then converted the results into teaching in the project with the ministry. Then it was back mainly to learning, from books and new experiences, from painful feedback and finally from Ina's story about reflective practice.

Apart from that, I was relatively autonomous and self-managing. In my best moments I adopted an open and 'learning' attitude and was able to collaborate constructively and learn. In my not-so-good moments I put that collaboration to the test, by not really listening to my colleagues' ideas and wishes and by letting my control and responsibility slip.

I am left with a satisfied feeling of a job well done and with the conviction that a book about learning is never finished and can never be finished – because then the learning is over!

Summary: self-managed learning and learning networks

Self-managed learning is a way of learning and working in which participants themselves plan, organise and implement their own learning activities.

Three skills needed for self-managed learning
- *Self-monitoring*: acquiring knowledge about one's own way of learning in relation to alternatives.
- *Self-direction*: taking action on the basis of the knowledge gained by self-monitoring.
- *Self-motivation*: generating one's own energy and motivation for learning.

Conditions for a context of self-managed learning
- Large degree of external structure in combination with wide internal freedom of choice.
- Castle and battlefield: safe learning climate and ambitious objectives.
- High motivation of participants in combination with hands-off attitude on the part of external parties.

An example of self-managed learning in learning groups is the *learning network*.

Principles of the learning network
- Participants are colleagues from the same organisation or professionals from different organisations.
- Learning activities arise on the basis of work questions and long-term objectives.
- Learning activities take place as close as possible to the workplace.
- The network controls and manages the group's learning itself.
- Control takes place in negotiation with control from management.
- Participants chart the learning objectives themselves, programme learning activities and participate in them.

Differences compared with peer consultation and project-based action learning
- Extension to other learning activities: planning and organising.
- Many actual learning activities take place outside the network.
- The facilitator or learning consultant of learning networks is relatively detached.
- The facilitator contributes expertise in the field of learning itself.
- All activities, and therefore the motivation to undertake these activities, must be provided by the participants themselves.

Summary: three forms of learning with colleagues
- Peer consultation groups learn separate from working.
- Project-based action learning groups learn in integration with working.
- Learning and meta-learning in learning networks is integrated with work.

Appendix A
Observation forms

A1 Binary observation form

How is the story put together?
- Consistent
- Broad outlines
- Clear
- Interesting
- Understandable
- Analytical

- Illogical
- Very detailed
- Confusing
- Dull
- Complicated
- Intuitive

How does the narrator describe his or her own position?
- Involved
- Active
- Dependent

- Detached
- Passive
- Independent

How does (s)he define relations with others?
- Collaboration
- Trust
- Leading
- Businesslike

- Conflict
- Distrust
- Following
- Personal

What is the tone of the story?
- Serious
- Prescriptive
- Self-assured

- Humorous
- Tentative
- Self-effacing

To what does (s)he apparently pay attention?
- Order, regularity
- Similarities
- Past
- What is fixed

- Spontaneity, ease
- Differences
- Future
- What is movable

A2 Multiple-choice observation form

Degree / Values	Not at all	To a small degree	More or less	Strongly	Very strongly
Ambition					
Tolerance					
Optimism					
Courage					
Forgiveness					
Helpfulness					
Honesty					
Compassion					
Sense of duty					
Respect					
Responsibility					
Control					
Collaboration					
Assertiveness					

Appendix B
Log books

B1 Participants log book

Subject	What comes easily to me	What I can improve on	Learning point/ learning moment	What I am going to practise next time
1.				
2.				
3.				
4.				
5.				
6.				

B2 Process facilitator's log book

Date:

Place:

Type of session / Working methods:

Present:

Name of issue holder and subjects discussed:

I am very pleased with:

I am less pleased with:

Who appeared to be primarily responsible (in other words: held a high 'valency') in this session for aspects such as

- Climate:
- Consideration:
- Support:
- Critical feedback:
- Quality control:

How I see the developmental stage of the group at present:

Appendix C
A mnemonic device for giving feedback: BOFF

The following technique, with the acronym 'BOFF', can be used when giving feedback.

C1 Critical feedback

B   *Step 1: Behaviour*
You give a description of the observable facts and behaviours and start the sentence with 'I'.
For example: 'I see your eyes drift and get the impression that you are not listening to me ...'

O   *Step 2: Outcome*
You say what feeling it evokes in yourself.
'... it gives me the feeling that you are not taking me seriously ...'

F   *Step 3: Feelings*
You say how you feel as a result.
'... and the consequence is that I feel less motivated to work with you.'

F   *Step 4: Future*
You describe behaviour that you would like to see in this situation.
'I would like it if you would make more of an effort to follow me.'

C2 Positive feedback

In the case of positive feedback, the final step is unnecessary:

B   *Step 1: Behaviour*
You provide a description of the observable facts and behaviours and start the sentence with 'I'.
For example: 'I find the way in which you tell that story very enthusiastic ...'

O   *Step 2: Outcome*

You say what response it evokes in yourself.

'... it makes me more enthusiastic myself ...'

F   *Step 3: Feelings*

You say how you feel as a result.

'... and the consequence is that am I keen to work with you on this project.'

Appendix D
Learning-style inventory

The learning-style inventory (LSI) evaluates the way you learn and how you deal with ideas and day-to-day situations in your life. We all have a sense that people learn in different ways, but this inventory will help you appreciate what 'learning style' can mean to you. It will help you to better understand:
- how you make career choices
- how you solve problems
- how you set goals
- how you manage others
- how you deal with new situations.

Instructions for completing the LSI

On page 189 you will be asked to complete 12 sentences. Each has four endings. Rank the endings for each sentence according to how well you think each one fits with how you would go about learning something. Try to recall some recent situations where you had to learn something new, perhaps in your job. Then, using the spaces provided, rank a '4' for the sentence ending that describes how you learn best, down to a '1' for the sentence ending that seems least like the way you learn. Be sure to rank all the endings for each sentence unit. Please do not make ties.

Scoring the LSI

1. When I learn: _1_ I am happy. _2_ I am fast. _3_ I am logical. _4_ I am careful.

Remember: 4 = most like you 3 = second most like you 2 = third most like you 1 = least like you

Record the score corresponding to the column letter (A–D) and the item number in the appropriate spaces indicated below. Total each row to get your final score for each of the four stages in the cycle of learning.

__ + __ + __ + __ + __ + __ + __ + __ + __ + __ + __ + __ = ☐
1A 2C 3D 4A 5A 6C 7B 8D 9B 10B 11A 12B   CE total

__ + __ + __ + __ + __ + __ + __ + __ + __ + __ + __ + __ = ☐
1D 2A 3C 4C 5B 6A 7A 8C 9A 10A 11B 12C   RO total

__ + __ + __ + __ + __ + __ + __ + __ + __ + __ + __ + __ = ☐
1B 2B 3A 4D 5C 6D 7C 8B 9D 10D 11C 12A   AC total

__ + __ + __ + __ + __ + __ + __ + __ + __ + __ + __ + __ = ☐
1C 2D 3B 4B 5D 6B 7D 8A 9C 10C 11D 12D   AE total

Now transfer the totals to the corresponding boxes on the next page.

The cycle of learning

There are four learning modes in the cycle of learning from experience: concrete experience (CE), reflective observation (RO), abstract conceptualisation (AC), and active experimentation (AE). Enter your total scores for each learning mode from the boxes above:

CE total ☐   RO total ☐   AC total ☐   AE total ☐

In the diagram on page 190, put a dot on each of the lines to correspond with your CE, RO, AC, and AE scores. Then connect the dots with a line so that you get a 'kite-like' shape. The shape and placement of this kite will show you which learning modes you tend to use most and which you use least.

The LSI is a simple test that helps you understand your strengths and weaknesses as a learner. It measures how much you rely on four different learning modes that are part of a four-stage cycle of learning. Different learners start at different places in this cycle. Effective learning uses each stage. You can see by the shape of your profile (above) which of the four learning modes you tend to prefer in a learning situation.[1]

1. One way to understand the meaning of your LSI scores better is to compare them with the scores of others. The profile gives norms on the four basic scales (CE, RO, AC, AE) for 1,446 adults ranging from 18 to 60 years of age. The sample group contained slightly more women

	A	B	C	D
1. When I learn:	— I like to deal with my feelings.	— I like to think about things.	— I like to be doing things.	— I like to watch and listen.
2. I learn best when:	— I listen and watch carefully.	— I rely on logical thinking.	— I trust my hunches and feelings.	— I work hard to get things done.
3. When I am learning:	— I tend to reason things out.	— I am responsible about things.	— I am quiet and reserved.	— I have strong feelings and reactions.
4. I learn by:	— feeling.	— doing.	— watching.	— thinking.
5. When I learn:	— I am open to new experiences.	— I look at all sides of issues.	— I like to analyse things, break them down into their parts.	— I like to try things out.
6. When I am learning:	— I am an observing person.	— I am an active person.	— I am an intuitive person.	— I am a logical person.
7. I learn best from:	— observation.	— personal relationships.	— rational theories.	— a chance to try out and practise.
8. When I learn:	— I like to see results from my work.	— I like ideas and theories.	— I take my time before acting.	— I feel personally involved in things.
9. I learn best when:	— I rely on my observations.	— I rely on my feelings.	— I can try things out for myself.	— I rely on my ideas.
10. When I am learning:	— I am a reserved person.	— I am an accepting person.	— I am a responsible person.	— I am a rational person.
11. When I learn:	— I get involved.	— I like to observe.	— I evaluate things.	— I like to be active.
12. I learn best when:	— I analyse ideas.	— I am receptive and open-minded.	— I am careful.	— I am practical.

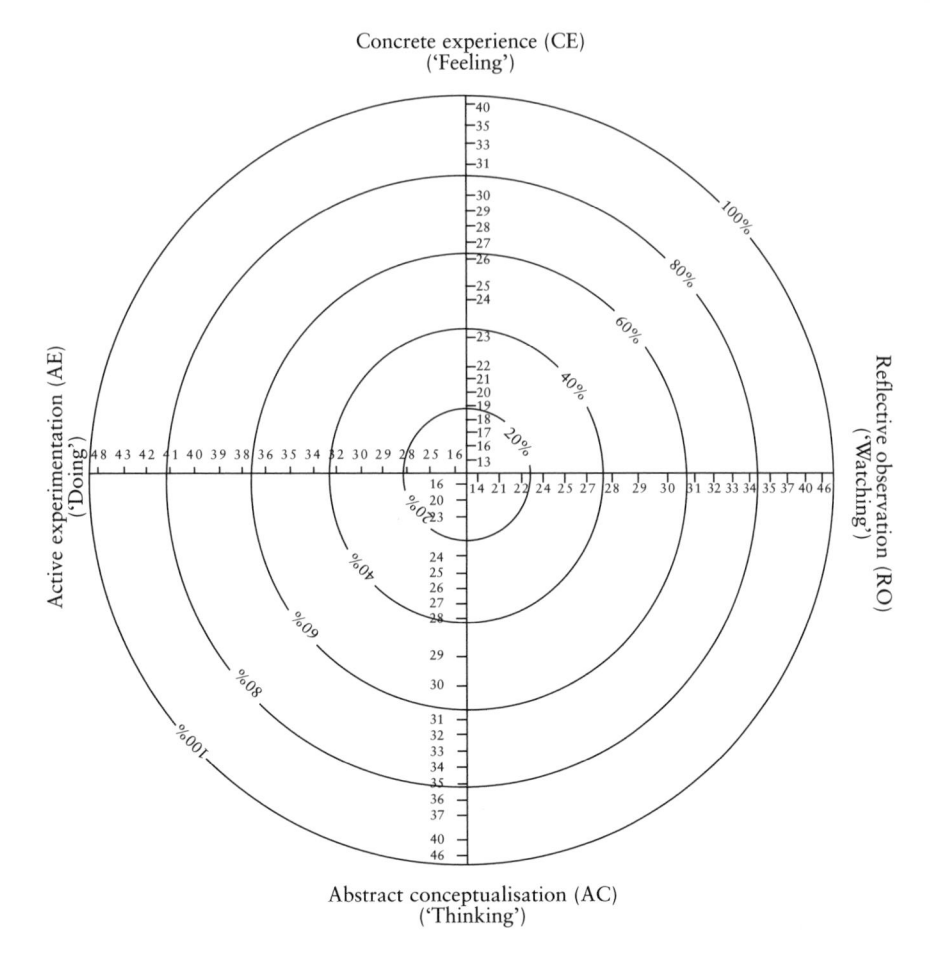

Concrete experience (CE)
('Feeling')

Active experimentation (AE)
('Doing')

Reflective observation (RO)
('Watching')

Abstract conceptualisation (AC)
('Thinking')

Remember:

1. The LSI gives you a general idea of how you view yourself as a learner.
2. Because learning is a cycle, the four stages occur time after time. While you are learning, you will probably repeat the cycle several times.
3. The LSI does not measure your learning skills with 100 per cent accuracy. You can find out more about how you learn by gathering information from other sources: your friends, instructors, and co-workers.

than men, with an average of two years beyond high school in formal education. A wide range of occupations and educational backgrounds is represented. The raw scores for each of the four basic scales are listed on the crossed lines of the target. The concentric circles on the target represent percentile scores for the normative group. In comparison to the normative group, the shape of your profile indicates which of the four basic modes you tend to emphasise most and which you emphasise least.

The four stages of the learning cycle and your learning strengths

Concrete Experience (CE)
This stage of the learning cycle emphasises personal involvement with people in everyday situations. In this stage, you would tend to rely more on your feelings than on a systematic approach to problems and situations. In a learning situation, you would rely on your ability to be open-minded and adaptable to change.

Learning from feeling
- Learning from specific experiences
- Relating to people
- Being sensitive to feelings and people

Reflective Observation (RO)
In this stage of the learning cycle, people understand ideas and situations from different points of view. In a learning situation you would rely on patience, objectivity, and careful judgment but would not necessarily take any action. You would rely on your own thoughts and feelings in forming opinions.

Learning by watching and listening
- Observing carefully before making judgments
- Viewing issues from different perspectives
- Looking for the meaning of things

Abstract Conceptualisation (AC)
In this stage, learning involves using logic and ideas, rather than feelings, to understand problems or situations. Typically, you would rely on systematic planning and develop theories and ideas to solve problems.

Learning by thinking
- Logically analysing ideas
- Systematic planning
- Acting on an intellectual understanding of a situation

Active Experimentation (AE)
Learning in this stage takes an active form: experimenting with influencing or changing situations. You would take a practical approach and be concerned with what really works, as opposed to simply watching a situation. You value getting things done and seeing the results of your influence and ingenuity.

Learning by doing
- Ability to get things done
- Risk-taking
- Influencing people and events through action

Learning style

From the preceding descriptions of concrete experience, reflective observation, abstract conceptualisation and active experimentation, you may have discovered that no single mode entirely describes your learning style. This is because each person's learning style is a combination of the four basic learning modes. Because of this, we are often pulled in several directions in a learning situation. By combining your scores, you can see which of four learning-style types best describes you. They are named as follows:

- Accommodator
- Diverger
- Converger
- Assimilator

Understanding your learning-style type – its strengths and weaknesses – is a major step toward increasing your learning power and getting the most from your learning experiences.

Learning-style type grid

Take your scores for the four learning modes, AC, CE, AE, and RO, listed earlier, and subtract as follows to get your two combination scores:

$$\boxed{} - \boxed{} = \boxed{} \qquad\qquad \boxed{} - \boxed{} = \boxed{}$$

AC   CE   AC–CE   AE   RO   AE–RO

A positive score on the AC–CE scale indicates that your score is more abstract. A negative score on the AC–CE scale indicates that your score is more concrete. Likewise, a positive or negative score on the AE-RO scale indicates that your scores are either more active or more reflective.

By marking your two combination scores, AC–CE and AE–RO, on the two lines of the grid opposite and plotting their point of interception, or data point, you can find which of the four learning styles you fall into. These four quadrants, labelled Accommodator, Diverger, Converger, and Assimilator, represent the four dominant learning styles.

The quadrant of the learning-style type grid into which your data point falls shows your preferred learning style. For example: If your AC–CE score was −8 and your AE–RO score was +15, your style would fall into the Accommodator quadrant. An AC–CE score of +7 and AE–RO score of +10 would fall into the Converger quadrant. The closer the data point is to the centre of the grid, the more balanced your learning style. If the data point falls near any of the far corners of the grid, you tend to rely heavily on one particular learning style.

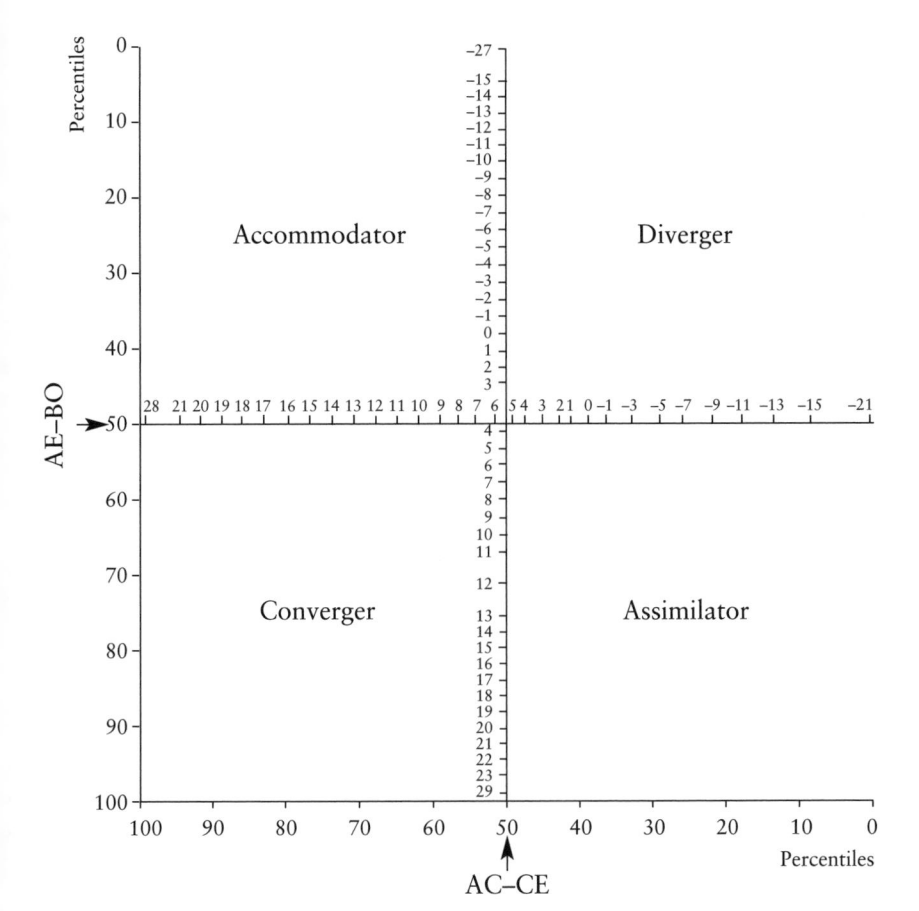

The four learning-style types[2]

Converger

Combines learning steps of *abstract conceptualisation* and *active experimentation*

People with this learning style are best at finding practical uses for ideas and theories. If this is your preferred learning style, you have the ability to solve problems and make decisions based on finding solutions to questions or problems. You would rather deal with technical tasks and problems than with social and interpersonal issues. These learning skills are important for effectiveness in specialist and technology careers.

Diverger

Combines learning steps of *concrete experience* and *reflective observation*

People with this learning style are best at viewing concrete situations from many different points of view. Their approach to situations is to observe rather than take action. If this is your style, you may enjoy situations that call for generating a wide range of ideas, as in brainstorming sessions. You probably have broad cultural interests and like to gather information. This imaginative ability and sensitivity to feelings is needed for effectiveness in arts, entertainment and service careers.

Assimilator

Combines learning steps of *abstract conceptualisation* and *reflective observation*

People with this learning style are best at understanding a wide range of information and putting it into concise, logical form. If this is your learning style, you are probably less focused on people and more interested in abstract ideas and concepts. Generally, people with this learning style find it more important that a theory have logical soundness than practical value. This learning style is important for effectiveness in information and science careers.

---

2. The learning-style inventory is based on several tested theories of thinking and creativity. The ideas behind assimilation and accommodation originate in Jean Piaget's definition of intelligence as the balance between the process of adapting concepts to fit the external world (accommodation) and the process of fitting observations of the world into existing concepts (assimilation). Convergence and divergence are the two essential creative processes identified by J. P. Guilford's structure-of-intellect model.

Accommodator

Combines learning steps of *concrete experience* and *active experimentation*

People with this learning style have the ability to learn primarily from 'hands-on' experience. If this is your style, you probably enjoy carrying out plans and involving yourself in new and challenging experiences. Your tendency may be to act on 'gut' feelings rather than on logical analysis. In solving problems, you may rely more heavily on people for information than on your own technical analysis. This learning style is important for effectiveness in action-oriented careers such as marketing or sales.

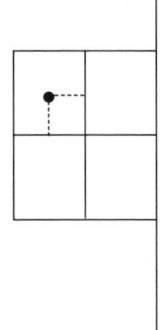

The importance of understanding your learning style

The ability to learn is the most important skill you can acquire. We are often confronted with new experiences or learning situations in life, in our careers, or on the job. In order to be an effective learner, you have to shift from getting involved (CE), to listening (RO), to creating an idea (AC), to making decisions (AE). As an adult, you have probably become better at some of these learning skills than others. You tend to rely on some skills and steps in the learning process more than others. As a result, you have developed a learning style.

Understanding your learning style helps you become aware of your strengths in some steps of the learning cycle. One way you can improve your learning effectiveness is to use those strengths when you are called upon to learn. More importantly, you can increase your effectiveness as a learner by improving your use of the steps you under-use.

Another way of understanding your learning style is to see how closely related it is to:

- choosing careers
- problem solving
- managing people
- working as part of a team.

On the following pages, you will:

- see how problem solving relates to learning styles
- learn how to improve your learning skills
- find out which careers are closely related to certain learning styles.

Using the learning cycle to help solve problems

Understanding your learning style can make you an effective problem solver. Nearly every problem that you encounter on the job or in your life involves the following skills:

- identifying the problem
- selecting the problem to solve
- seeing different solutions
- evaluating possible results
- implementing the solution.

Different pieces of the problem must be approached in different ways. Look back at your strengths and weaknesses in the four learning modes. Compare them with the problem-solving model illustrated on the next page. If you rely heavily on concrete experience, you may find that you can easily identify problems that need to be worked on or solved. However, you may need to increase your ability to evaluate possible solutions, as in abstract conceptualisation. Or you may find that your strong points rest with carrying out or implementing solutions, as in active experimentation. If this is so, you may need to work on carefully selecting the problem, as in reflective observation.

Comparison of the learning cycle with problem-solving skills

The next section contains strategies to help you develop your learning skills.

Improving your learning and problem-solving skills

You can improve your ability to learn and solve problems in three ways:
1. Develop learning and work relationships with people whose learning strengths and weaknesses are opposite to yours.
2. Improve the fit between your learning-style strengths and the kinds of learning and problem-solving experiences you face.
3. Practise and develop learning skills in your areas of weakness.

First strategy

Develop supportive relationships. This is the easiest way to improve your learning skills. Recognise your own learning-style strengths and build on them. At the same time, value other people's different learning styles. Also, do not assume that you have to solve problems alone. Learning power is increased by working with others. Although you may be drawn to people who have similar learning skills, you will learn more and experience the learning cycle more fully with friends and co-workers who have opposite learning skills.

How? If you have an abstract learning style, like a Converger, you can learn to communicate ideas more effectively by associating with people who are more concrete and people-oriented, like Divergers. A person with a more reflective style can benefit from observing the risk-taking and active experimentation of someone who is more active, like an Accommodator.

Second strategy

Improve the match or fit between your learning style and your life situation. This is a more difficult way to achieve better learning performance and life satisfaction.

How? There are a number of ways to do this. For some people, this may mean a change of career or job to a new field where they feel more at home with the values and skills required of them. Most people, however, can improve the match between their learning style and tasks by reorganising their priorities and activities. They can concentrate on those tasks and activities that lie in their areas of learning strength and rely on other people in their areas of learning weakness.

Third strategy

Become a flexible learner. You can do this by strengthening the learning skills in which you are weak. This strategy is the most challenging, but is also the most rewarding. By becoming flexible, you will be able to cope with problems of all kinds and will be more adaptable in changing situations. Because this is more difficult, it involves more time and tolerance for your own mistakes and failure.

How?
1. Develop a long-term plan. Look for improvements and payoffs over months and years, rather than right away.
2. Look for safe opportunities to practise new skills. Find situations that test your new skills but will not punish you for failure.
3. Reward yourself – becoming a flexible learner is hard work.

The chart below identifies the strengths and weaknesses of each learning style with notes for improvement.

Concrete experience

ACCOMODATOR		DIVERGER	
Strengths:	Getting things done Leadership Risk-taking	Strengths:	Imaginative ability Understanding people Recognising problems Brainstorming
Too much:	Trivial improvements Meaningless activity	Too much:	Paralysed by alternatives Can't make decisions
Not enough:	Work not completed on time Impractical plans Not directed to goals	Not enough:	No ideas Can't recognise problems and opportunities

To develop your Accommodative learning skills, practise:
* Committing yourself to objectives
* Seeking new opportunities
* Influencing and leading others
* Being personally involved
* Dealing with people

To develop your Divergent learning skills, practise:
* Being sensitive to people's feelings
* Being sensitive to values
* Listening with an open mind
* Gathering information
* Imagining the implications of uncertain situations

Active
experimentation ———————————————————— *Reflective*
                                      observation

CONVERGER		ASSIMILATOR	
Strengths:	Problem-solving Decision making Deductive reasoning Defining problems	Strengths:	Planning Creating models Defining problems Developing theories
Too much:	Solving the wrong problem Hasty decision-making	Too much:	Castles in the air No practical application
Not enough:	Lack of focus No shifting of ideas Scattered thoughts	Not enough:	Unable to learn from mistakes No sound basis for work No systematic approach

To develop your Convergent learning skills, practise:
* Creating new ways of thinking and doing
* Experimenting with new ideas
* Choosing the best solution
* Setting goals
* Making decisions

To develop your Assimilative learning skills, practise:
* Organising information
* Building conceptual models
* Testing theories and ideas
* Designing experiments
* Analysing quantitative data

Abstract conceptualisation

Review the Career Map below. See how well your learning style matches your job.

Concrete experience

ACCOMODATOR	DIVERGER

Careers in organisations
Fields: Management
Public administration
Education
Administration
Banking

Jobs: Accountant
Manager/supervisor
Administrator

Careers in business and promotion fields:
Fields: Marketing
Government Business
Retail

Jobs: Salesperson/retailer
Politician
Public relations specialist
General manager

Careers in Arts and Entertainment
Fields: Literature Theatre
Television Journalism

Jobs: Actor/Actress
Musician Athlete
Artist Designer

Careers in Service Organisations
Fields: Social Work
Psychology
Police
Nursing

Jobs: Counselor/therapist
Social worker
Personnel manager
Planner
Management consultant

Active — — — — — — — — — — — — — — *Reflective*
experimentation | *observation*

CONVERGER	ASSIMILATOR

Careers as specialists
Fields: Mining Forestry
Farming Economics

Jobs: Civil engineer
Chemical engineer
Production supervisor

Careers in Technology
Fields: Engineering
Computer science
Medicine
Physical science

Jobs: Physician
Engineer
Computer programmer
Medical technician
Applied scientist
Industrial salesperson
Manager

Careers in Information
Fields: Education
Sociology
Ministry
Law

Jobs: Teacher Writer
Librarian Minister
College professor

Careers in Science
Fields: Mathematics
Physical science
Biology

Jobs: Planner
R&D scientist
Academic physician
Researcher
Financier

Abstract conceptualisation

Resources for further study

Experiential Learning: Experience as the Source of Learning and Development, by David A. Kolb (Englewood Cliffs, NJ: Prentice-Hall, 1984). The theory of experiential learning, with applications to education, work, and personal development. Contains information on the validity of the learning-atyle inventory.

User Guide for the Learning-Style Inventory, by Donna Smith and David A. Kolb (Boston: McBer & Company, 1985). A manual for teachers and trainers.

Personal Learning Guide, by Richard Baker, Nancy Dixon and David A. Kolb (Boston: McBer & Company, 1985). A practical guide to using training programs to increase learning.

Adaptive Style Inventory, by Experience Based Learning, David A. Kolb and Richard Boyatzis (distributed by McBer & Company, Boston, MA 02116). An inventory to assess your adaptability in different learning situations.

Learning Skills Profile, by Experience Based Learning, David A. Kolb and Richard Boyatzis (distributed by McBer & Company, Boston, MA 02116). An instrument to compare your learning skills to your job skill demands.

Bibliography of Research on Experiential Learning and the Learning-Style Inventory (Boston: McBer & Company, updated 1992).

Appendix E
Research into peer consultation: how do participants learn?

Introduction

Peer consultation is a way of learning with fellow professionals that is gaining in popularity. In peer consultation groups, professionals submit issues from their work for practical and systematic discussion with their colleagues. Peer consultation is regarded by many consultants as an optimal method for connecting 'learning' and 'working'. Peer consultation sessions are therefore focused on concrete issues and often take place within the participants' place of work.

This study examines whether the promise of peer consultation is indeed realised:

- Do the participating professionals actually learn during these sessions?
- If so, what type of learning do professionals report?
- Does this type of learning affect the way in which professionals work?

Altogether, 126 participants in peer consultation groups participated in the study, which was used to study the following research question:

- What are the demonstrable learning effects of peer consultation for the participating professionals?

And the more specific sub-question:

- To what extent does peer consultation stimulate the four different learning styles: divergent, convergent, accommodative and assimilative?

These questions are explored by means of a study that is partly quantitative and partly qualitative. We use a questionnaire containing 35 closed questions which we send to (former) participants in peer consultation with a view to exploring the subjectively observed learning effects. The additional tools we use are one open question, interviews with peer consultation facilitators and

Table 1 *An overview of all items belonging to the different learning scales*

Learning scales	Item	Question
Divergent	6	'In action learning, I receive valuable feedback from the other participants.'
	8	'In action learning, I recognise a great deal of myself in issues submitted by others.'
	9	'In action learning, my perspective on issues changes as a result of considering the viewpoints of others.'
	11	'In action learning, I learn to concentrate on the crux of the issue at hand.'
	12	'In action learning, the methods used produce in-depth exploration of issues.'
	15	'As a result of action learning, I have become alert to the questions underlying the issue.'
	17	'As a result of action learning, I have greater insight into the strong points of my performance.'
	19	'As a result of action learning, I have greater insight into the weaker points of my performance.'
Assimilative	7	'In action learning, I learn to link things to knowledge gained previously.'
	13	'In action learning, I gain new knowledge.'
Accommodative	10	'In action learning, I gain experience with a new form of learning.'
	20	'As a result of action learning, my contacts with clients/customers/managers have improved.'
Convergent	14	'As a result of action learning, I am following new routes in my work.'
	16	'As a result of action learning, I am applying new ideas to my work.'
	18	'As a result of action learning, I have changed my ways of working.'

attendance at peer consultation sessions. The questionnaire covers Kolb's four learning styles (Table 1).
There are six independent variables:
1. the person who takes the initiative towards participation in peer consultation
2. the degree to which it is considered important to engage in reflection at work
3. time spent in a peer consultation group
4. number of peer consultation sessions attended
5. value attributed to the peer consultation process
6. individual expectations of self-efficacy.

The last of these is useful in assessing the relationship between participants' learning styles and their expectations about their own success or failure in dealing with difficult situations. Research by Anderson and Betz (2001) shows that individuals' expectations about their self-efficacy directly influence their personal and career development. Personal self-efficacy expectations are often regarded as primary determinants of behavioural change (Sherer and Maddux, 1982). Individuals with high self-efficacy are more flexible and more determined to cope with difficult situations. Self-efficacy expectations appear to determine an individual's initial decision to behave in a certain way. They also determine how much effort individuals put in, as well as their staying power when they are confronted with obstacles (Sherer and Maddux, 1982). Earlier research shows that self-efficacy plays a central role in the effectiveness of training courses and the transfer to practice (Bandura, 1982; Saks, 1997).

Results

Characterisation of participants
To establish the starting position of the participants in this study, we first examine the distribution of frequencies and percentages over all categories of responses for the five independent variables. See Table 2 for an overview.

Reliability of the scales
The internal consistency of all of our scales is presented in Table 3. The items within the divergent, convergent and assimilative learning styles show a fairly high correlation (alpha = .64), especially given the low number of items. The internal consistency within the accommodative learning style (alpha = .47) can be described as low; thus no conclusions can be drawn about this learning style. Self-efficacy is measured by means of the existing questionnaire adapted by Teeuw, Schwarzer and Jerusalem (1994). The ten items on this questionnaire show an internal consistency of .79. This is

Table 2 *Distribution of frequencies and percentages over all response categories per independent variable*

Independent variables	Response categories	Frequencies	%
Date of starting peer consultation (N = 126)	In past 3 months	14	11.1
	3–12 months ago	33	26.2
	1–2 years ago	60	47.6
	>3 years ago	19	15.1
Currently part of a peer consultation group? (N= 126)	Yes	91	72.2
	No	35	27.8
Started peer consultation on (N= 126)	Own initiative	63	50
	Employer's initiative	63	50
Number of sessions attended (N= 126)	<4	29	23
	4–8	48	38.1
	>8	49	38.9
Is reflection at work important? (N= 126)	No, definitely not	0	0
	No, hardly	4	3.2
	Yes, to some extent	33	26.2
	Yes, definitely	88	69.8
	No response	1	0.8

Each respondent also allocates a mark to the peer consultation process as a whole. All scores are between 5 and 9, with a mean of 7.4 (standard deviation: 0.73).

slightly lower than in previous studies, in which alpha varied between .81 and .91, but can certainly be described as high.

Unfortunately the results show that the correlation between the different learning style scales is also fairly high (correlations are between .36 and .65, with $p<.01$: see Table 3). This is due to the fact that the respondents generally report a large number of learning effects, and therefore show a positive score on most items. Therefore we should be careful when drawing conclusions about the learning styles themselves. Replication studies with respect to the scales are required and it is recommended that additional items be included, for the accommodative learning style in particular. The correlations in Table 3 also show that the learning style scales are independent of the self-efficacy scale.

How do participants learn?

As described in Chapter 19, based on Kolb's (1984) theory on experiential learning, we expect participants in peer consultation to learn primarily in

Table 3 *Mean values, standard deviations, internal consistencies and correlations of the scales used*

Scales	N	No. of items	M	SD	Alpha	Correlation coefficients					
						Divergent learning style	Assimilative learning style	Accommodative learning style	Convergent learning style	Self-efficacy
Divergent learning style	126	8	3.31	0.31	0.75	1.00				
Assimilative learning style	126	2	3.28	0.38	0.64	0.56*	1.00			
Accommodative learning style	126	2	3.20	0.51	0.47	0.44*	0.36*	1.00		
Convergent learning style	124	3	2.91	0.60	0.79	0.65*	0.54*	0.53*	1.00	
Self-efficacy	124	10	2.70	0.57	0.79	−0.05	0.08	−0.12	0.40	1.00

* p < .01

a divergent manner. This means that during peer consultation they mainly observe and reflect on concrete situations. We therefore expect the assimilative, convergent and accommodative learning styles to receive relatively little attention.

Participants score mainly on 'divergence'
It appears that it is important to be cautious when drawing conclusions based on the learning styles measured. More reliable statements about our research question may be obtained by examining participants' response tendencies. To explore which aspects of peer consultation appeal to participants more than others, we divide participants' scores on the items into high, medium high, medium low and low scores (see Table 4). We observe that the scores for items with low and high scores vary with more than one standard deviation. Based on this table we can conclude that, according to the participants, peer consultation mainly addresses the type of learning described in Items 6, 11 and 12. These items represent a specific type of divergent learning: participants feel that they receive valuable feedback from other participants as part of peer consultation; that they learn to concentrate on the crux of the issue submitted; and that they learn to explore issues in depth using certain methods. Items 16, 18 and 20 describe the type of learning that is least addressed in peer consultation according to the participants. This relates particularly to learning in a convergent manner. This style involves the application of new ideas and the adjustment of one's own way of working as a result of peer consultation. Participants also

Table 4 *Means and standard deviations on all items (scales) divided into high, medium high, medium low and low scores*

	Scales	Items	M	SD	N
High scores (> 3.4)	Divergence	Item 6	3.51	0.52	126
		Item 11	3.45	0.61	126
		Item 12	3.54	0.54	126
	Self-efficacy	Item 22	3.40	0.53	125
		Item 27	3.50	0.48	125
		Item 31	3.50	0.52	125
Medium high scores (between 3.1 and 3.4)	Assimilation	Item 7	3.20	0.57	126
		Item 13	3.21	0.62	126
	Divergence	Item 8	3.35	0.58	126
		Item 9	3.25	0.68	126
		Item 15	3.19	0.67	126
	Accommodation	Item 10	3.25	0.72	126
	Self-efficacy	Item 23	3.10	0.45	125
		Item 24	3.20	0.52	125
		Item 25	3.30	0.59	125
		Item 26	3.30	0.57	125
		Item 28	3.30	0.57	125
		Item 29	3.20	0.59	125
		Item 30	3.20	0.45	124
Medium low scores (between 2.8 and 3.1)	Divergence	Item 17	2.94	0.67	126
		Item 19	3.06	0.72	126
	Convergence	item 14	2.80	0.66	125
Low scores (< 2.8)	Accommodation	Item 20	2.58	0.77	126
	Convergence	Item 16	2.74	0.72	126
		Item 18	2.56	0.66	125

Based on the following response categories: 1 = No, definitely not; 2 = No, hardly; 3 = Yes, to some extent; 4 = Yes, definitely.

report that peer consultation has relatively little influence on improving their contacts with clients, managers or customers.

Summary of quantitative results

Due to the limitations of this study, we refer only to the presence or absence of significant *indications* and not to *observed effects*. Our results are as follows:

1. Indications that participants mainly learn in a divergent manner in peer

Table 5 *Correlation between some of the independent variables and the reported learning effects (for various learning styles)*

	Number of sessions (<4 vs. >8)	Currently part of a peer consultation group?	Reflection at work is important?	Appreciation for own peer consultation process
Divergence	0.45**	0.21*	0.23**	0.49**
Assimilation	0.11	0.04	0.22*	0.35**
Accommodation	0.24**	0.05	0.16	0.34**
Convergence	0.27**	0.24**	0.26**	0.45**
Self-efficacy	0.05	0.11	0.02	0.04

* $p < .05$; ** $p < .01$

consultation. Three particular aspects of divergent learning are involved here (see Table 4).
- Participants feel that they receive valuable feedback from other participants during peer consultation.
- Participants learn to concentrate on the crux of the issues at hand.
- Participants learn to explore issues in depth, using certain methods.

2. Indications that convergent learning in particular receives relatively little attention in peer consultation. The following aspects are involved (Table 4):
- Participants report minimal application of new ideas to their own work.
- Participants adjust their own working methods very little as a result of peer consultation.
- Participants report minimal improvement in contacts with clients, managers and customers as a result of peer consultation.

3. Indications that there is increase in learning effects when more peer consultation sessions are attended. These are indirect indications, because we compare between subjects (see Table 5).
- Participants who attended more than eight peer consultation sessions report significantly more divergent and convergent learning than participants who attended fewer than four sessions.

4. Few indications of own initiative or self-efficacy as a relevant dimension.
- No differences in reported learning between participants who took the initiative to attend peer consultation and participants who join peer consultation groups as a result of their employer's initiative.
- Expectations of self-efficacy of participants appear to have no influence on reported learning effects (see Tables 3 and 5).

5. The response to three filter questions resulted in a significant effect:
    -   Participants who are currently in a peer consultation group report significantly more divergent and convergent learning effects than participants who have completed the process (see Table 5). This is consistent with findings about the transfer of learning as described in literature on training (see e.g. Broad and Newstrom, 1992).
    -   Participants who find reflection with colleagues at work more important than others report more divergent and convergent learning effects (see Table 5). These participants also give the entire peer consultation process a higher mark.
    -   Participants who give a higher mark to the entire peer consultation process report significantly more learning effects (see Table 5).

Summary of qualitative results

In the qualitative remarks and comments that supplement the closed questions of the questionnaire, the subjects emphasise the 'frank', 'positively confrontational' nature of peer consultation and the importance they attach to maintaining the sense of security in the group and mutual trust and respect (see de Haan and de Ridder, 2003). We regard this as additional confirmation that peer consultation groups mainly involve divergent learning, because divergent learning appeals to emotions, mutual relationships between people, and sensitivity for others (Kolb, 1984). What also stands out is the fact that participants report that results are often not directly applicable in practice (see de Haan and de Ridder, 2003), which is another indication of the lesser role of convergence and accommodation in peer consultation.

Conclusion

In response to the question that is the title of this appendix ('How do participants learn?'), a picture seems to emerge of a learning group that learns most during peer consultation sessions, and mainly by exploring issues in depth and receiving personal feedback. Divergent learning seems to reign.

Generally speaking, this confirms the findings of Driehuis (1997), who also emphasises reflecting and divergent learning. In addition, Driehuis' report indicates a positive 'impulse to redirect one's own actions'. However, we find extremely low scores on the items geared to redirecting one's own actions (Items 14, 16 and 18: see Table 4). If we look more closely, however, we see that Driehuis finds primarily an 'intention to redirect one's actions' and an 'expected redirecting of others', while true 'experimentation with redirecting own actions' clearly scores lower. Driehuis too finds few indications of accommodative learning.

Appendix F
A peer consultation community: action learning at the BBC[1]

The following pages are inspired very much by a tradition in the action learning literature, of facilitators and participants taking reflections on their experience in action learning a step further by writing about them. David Casey and David Pearce have edited a book of experiences with action learning in General Electric in the 1970s (Casey and Pearce, 1973). Pedler (1983) has brought together a wide variety of impressions and experiences from action learning initiatives, and Yury Boshyk has edited two books of 'best practices' and 'experiences of leadership development' through action learning (Boshyk 2000 and 2002). It is interesting to read these publications and see how they breathe the same inquisitive and reflective spirit found in action learning – a congruence of form and subject matter that we hope to echo in this appendix.

We will describe an action learning initiative that is a cornerstone of a large-scale leadership development programme in an organisation which aspires to be a world leader in creativity and innovation. As this initiative is still unfolding and will continue for another four years, our results can only be very preliminary. However, our shared excitement and learning are already well under way and it seems timely to reflect on and share what we have found to date.

Co-creating change

'The BBC Leadership Programme is one of a number of key change initiatives arising from a major shift in thinking at the BBC', believes Ian Hayward, Head of Leadership Development at the Corporation. Key to this change is the BBC Making it Happen initiative, which included a large group event involving 10,000 employees. The shared vision is to make the BBC 'the

1. I would like to thank Ian Hayward (Head of Leadership Development at the BBC), Will Perry (Head of Action Learning at the BBC), and Kathleen King and Caryn Vanstone, Business Directors at Ashridge Consulting, for valuable contributions to this Appendix.

most creative organisation in the world'. A clear message from employees was that in order for this to happen, there was a need for stronger leadership at every level of the organisation.

In the past, the BBC was focused more on 'managing' than on 'leading' others, and on process rather than on creativity. The working structure was systems driven, dominated by committee-based decision making and bureaucratic procedures. The whole organisation had become too internally competitive and compartmentalised. The need for a new leadership approach was clear.

However, whilst wishing to release more creativity and innovation, the BBC – especially since the 2003–4 Hutton inquiry – needs to demonstrate accountability, efficiency and trustworthiness in the eyes of the public, as it approaches its Charter Review in 2006.

In June 2002, BBC Training and Development invited tenders for a leadership development programme from a number of top UK business schools. In response, Ashridge Consulting and Ashridge Executive Education worked together to blend the best of their different approaches and skills. This produced a tender that incorporated innovative ideas for co-design and co-delivery; practical and intellectually rigorous content; and a challenging approach to leadership development based on leading-edge complexity thinking (Shaw, 2002).

In September 2003, the first group of BBC managers embarked on the BBC Leadership Programme within Ashridge. This was the start of a unique leadership and development initiative aimed at nurturing creativity, accountability and trust. Based on the principles of action learning and inquiry, this programme will be experienced by around 6,000 leaders over the next four to five years. The key informing principles guiding the design of the learning process, and the specific leadership models it offers, include the following:

- Increased diversity, and reduction of power differentials will be vital to improve innovation and creativity.
- Creativity emerges through contention and mess, and therefore leaders have to learn how to handle the dilemma of needing to be both clear and uncertain at the same time.

The design features a series of events and learning processes spread out over a six-month period. A group of 120 leaders is selected from across divisions and levels of hierarchy. All engage in a 360° feedback process before starting the programme. A first workshop brings them together in a large group event over two days. During this time they develop their skills of inquiry and action/reflection based learning. This is facilitated through a process designed to explore with them the BBC's own unique context and ecology – and how this impacts on their orientation and choices as leaders.

This is followed by a smaller three-day workshop for 15–20 peers – senior leaders, established leaders and team leaders. These workshops across three pathways all cover essential skills such as leading high performance and creativity, and coaching-based leadership, while they place different accents on topics such as diversity, strategy and managing complexity.

After the workshops, the six-month learning process is supported using a mixture of action learning groups, coaching, on-line modules and work-based projects – all designed to facilitate organisational as well as personal development.

Finally, all 120 leaders participating in a programme come together again to share their learning, explore new areas of interest and explore together how they might continue their learning. At this stage participants may volunteer to become coaches, action learning facilitators and mentors to future programmes. Thus the programme aims to build an increasing sustainability of learning support inside the BBC itself.

A peer consultation initiative

As can be seen from the above, the practice of peer consultation has informed the design and delivery of the BBC Leadership Programme in different ways:

- Internal leadership development consultants from the BBC seek consultation with their peers from Ashridge.
- Facilitation of all medium to large group events (e.g. the opening and the pathway workshops) was done by colleagues from three organisations (BBC Leadership Development, Ashridge College and Ashridge Consulting) working in close consultation.
- Participants of the programme are invited and encouraged to take on coaching or facilitating roles within the Leadership Programme and afterwards, thus becoming peers of the programme facilitators.
- Last but not least – action learning is a key element in the leadership development process, and has even been described by some participants as the single most impactful learning experience.

Structure of the action learning community

Action learning within the BBC leadership programme is a large-scale project. At the time of writing Programmes 1–6 are ongoing, and 'only' 631 BBC leaders have commenced with the programme. From these first six programmes, there are now 545 people in 102 action learning sets, an uptake of around 86 per cent. There are 40 facilitators involved, 29 from Ashridge and 11 from the BBC. Attendance figures to all four sessions seem to range from 60–80 per cent. All these numbers have been growing over the past nine months, since the start of the action learning initiative, and are all still growing.

How does one facilitate a community of this scale, and how does one 'manage' this large community of action learners and facilitators, without threatening key pre-conditions like freedom, safety, confidence and trust, or even the quality of learning itself, which can be jeopardised so easily by rigid management structures and procedures?

Within the BBC Leadership Programme, a number of different routes were taken in parallel:

- Offering participants freedom in signing up to action learning, determining the agenda of their action learning sessions, and taking away the learning on their own terms.
- Encouraging participants with a special interest and enthusiasm for action learning to facilitate within their own sets and beyond the programme – for example, facilitating action learning groups in future Leadership Programmes.
- Entrusting a team of BBC colleagues, one of them an experienced action learning facilitator, with the care and coordination of the action learning support structure.
- Stimulating and training new action learning facilitators, applying agreed and transparent quality standards.

From the perspective of action learning participants

The action learner need not be bothered too much by the underlying philosophy and objectives. Our aim is to let participants experience action learning as quickly and directly as possible. So, after a brief introduction to the history and scope of action learning, the participants of every pathway workshop experience action learning in the last afternoon, in the form of a 'taster session'. After that, participants receive the information in the box on the next page ('Getting started') and have the opportunity to sign up to an action learning group with limited scope (four sessions). An overwhelming majority chooses to do this.

From the perspective of action learning facilitators

The action learning facilitators receive a reader with recommended approaches to peer consultation, the 'Getting Started' box below, some sheets to monitor attendance and, after several months, a request to report back on general and strictly non-attributable organisational themes.

Experienced facilitators from either the BBC or Ashridge who wish to become action learning facilitators, are required to make themselves thoroughly acquainted with action learning facilitation. Our action learning facilitators' training is designed with the following success criteria in mind:

- There is a robust resource allocation system, so that all groups share facilitator availability.
- The BBC provides highly skilled facilitators who enhance the learning process.
- Skills development opportunities are provided for internal BBC facilitators through taking on the role of action learning facilitator.
- BBC and Ashridge action learning facilitators use learning processes to

Action learning: getting started

1. Your workshop tutor will allocate you an action learning facilitator and a choice of dates for your first meeting.
2. Action learning meetings will involve a total of four half days. These can take place over two full days or four half days, or a mixture. As a group, decide which date is most suitable.
3. If the group cannot make any of the dates proposed by the facilitator, they should together decide on one date (full or half day) where they can all meet together and contact the facilitator to see if they are able to make the new date.
4. Once you have agreed a date, nominate a group representative who will email the facilitator and the other members of the group, to inform them of the chosen date, the member's names, and whether the first meeting will be for one day or half a day. *This needs to be done within one week of the workshop. Please copy this email to the Action Learning Co-ordinator.*
5. The representative also needs to book a room for the first meeting and inform the facilitator and members of the group. Please note that there is no budget to pay for room bookings. Should action learning groups have difficulty finding a room, there are syndicate rooms available at BBC Training & Development – please call the Action Learning Co-ordinator if one is needed.
6. If the facilitator cannot make the new date please contact the Action Learning Co-ordinator, who will find another facilitator

enhance their skills, and provide high-quality organisational data back to the BBC.

The procedure for becoming an action learning facilitator is outlined in the box on the following page ('Becoming a facilitator').

As a means of support to the action learning facilitators and also as a way to hear back from the many action learning sessions which take place across the BBC, we have started monthly action learning cafes which are open to all action learning facilitators working on the Leadership Programme.

The purpose of these action learning cafes is
- to reflect in action learning format on issues arising from facilitating action learning groups
- to refresh facilitators' approaches by offering new and different ways of working with action learning sets
- to enjoy and reflect on 'good conversation' within a group of peers committed to a common project.

Action learning: becoming a facilitator

1. We build a pool of internal and external (i.e. BBC and Ashridge) trainers and facilitators who are interested in contributing as action learning facilitators.
2. BBC Assessment and Development assesses individuals from the pool and gives a recommendation: 'ready to start', 'ready for training', 'not sufficiently prepared'.
3. The facilitators with recommendation 'ready for training' are booked into one of four 'action learning facilitation development days' for 8–16 delegates. These 'development days' are facilitated by experienced facilitators from Ashridge Consulting, and consist of
   - pre-reading
   - one day of practice as clients and consultants (morning) and as facilitators (afternoon)
   - two months of practice facilitating one or two action learning groups, and
   - a half-day follow-up session in action learning format, where issues are taken from action learning practice and participants self-facilitate the action learning (with the trainers acting as coaches to the group).
4. All action learning facilitators are expected to go to a 'concepts and models induction workshop', which further familiarizes them with the BBC Leadership Programme, its objectives, concepts and working methodology.
5. Further support structures include:
   - individual support from the action learning facilitation trainers (on request)
   - monthly 'action learning cafes' run as consultation groups, where the topic is '(facilitation of) action learning within the Leadership Programme' (see below)
   - dedicated action learning programme coordinators and administrators within Ashridge Consulting and BBC Training and Development.

These action learning cafes were designed as a flexible learning community. The design discards Revans' original idea of the closed set as a vehicle for action learning, and introduces the alternative idea of a peer consultation community around a certain topic – in this case the topic is '(facilitation of) action learning within the Leadership Programme'. A similar design with open sets was introduced by Ray Mahoney for the Corporation of London (Weinstein, 2002).

Figure A.1 provides a graphical depiction of the 'learning loop' of action learning for every pathway workshop of the Leadership Programme. Action learning facilitators receive this overview.

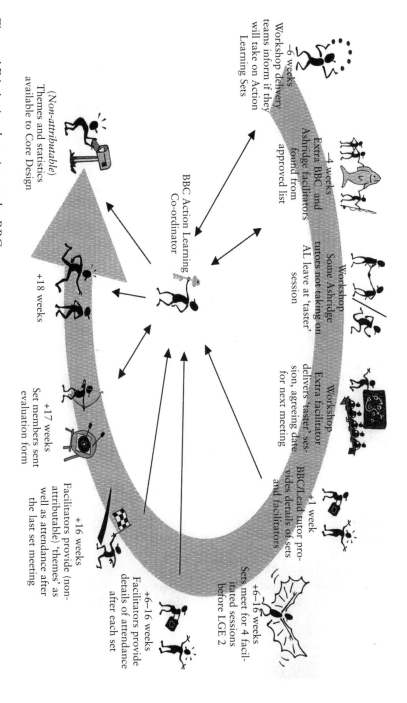

Figure AF.1 *Action learning at the BBC*

−6 weeks
Workshop delivery teams inform if they will take on Action Learning Sets

−6 weeks
Workshop
Extra BBC and Ashridge facilitators found from approved list

−4 weeks
Workshop
Some Ashridge tutors not taking on AL leave at 'taster' session

Workshop
Extra facilitator delivers 'taster' session, agreeing date for next meeting

BBC Action Learning Co-ordinator

+1 week
BBC/Lead tutor provides details of sets and facilitators

+6–16 weeks
Sets meet for 4 facilitated sessions before LGE 2

+6–16 weeks
Facilitators provide details of attendance after each set

+16 weeks
Facilitators provide (non-attributable) 'themes' as well as attendance after the last set meeting

+17 weeks
Set members sent evaluation form

+18 weeks
(*Non-attributable*)
Themes and statistics available to Core Design

Generally, we try to work with an abundance of 'support mechanisms' and as few 'management systems' as possible, in order to encourage action learners and facilitators to find their own way of learning, and to adapt methodology to the multiplicity of issues and concerns that arise at the start of every action learning endeavour. This way of 'fostering' the action learning with as much freedom as possible, balancing this freedom with clear commitments and responsibilities, has led to a flourish of activity but also to somewhat disappointing attendance figures, which we are looking into. We are proceeding in the spirit of the Leadership Programme – to inform participants and facilitators (about the consequences of low attendance) and to inquire with participants and facilitators about the reason for non-attendance, trying to understand the dynamic whereby some group members join voluntarily but do not turn up at action learning sessions.

Some early observations

The BBC is an organisation with generally highly trained professionals, many of whom are operating at the limits of their professional field of expertise. The organisation has a particularly high track record in professional development, coaching and training – supported by state-of-the-art HR systems such as an internal coaching function and a virtual learning resource centre. In many respects the BBC, even before Making it Happen, could have been described as a 'learning organisation' if ever there was one, both in terms of collective curricula as well as individual development of its staff. All those involved in the design and implementation of the Leadership Programme have been aware of this and of the need to leave the responsibility for learning as much as possible with the individual participants to whom we aim to offer relevant and challenging learning experiences.

Peer consultation is eminently suitable to this kind of organisation, precisely because participants in action learning:

- focus on their own specific concerns and issues and
- learn from each other, in other words by drawing prompts for change and innovation from peers whom they respect as experienced and capable of handling similar issues.

As we have expected, action learning is generally encountering very positive responses from leaders within the BBC. Some specific outcomes based on the first evaluations are as follows:

- Many action learners are struggling with aspects of leadership styles that they are experiencing. One of the ascriptions we sometimes hear is that of the 'bully' – the leader who has a 'command style' approach. Not only do participants share in action learning what it means to be on the receiving end of a 'bully', but they also discover what has created this style of leadership. They even sometimes see the 'bully within themselves' or their own 'passive aggression', thanks to the practice of action learning to inquire about the issue holder's own share in his or her issue.

- Many action learners are finding out about the dynamic of 'maximising professional freedom' while 'imposing hard and immovable deadlines'. They discover how they are themselves sometimes putting impossible demands on the organisation and its leadership.
- Some uncomfortable features associated with self-discovery include the following:
  - action learning turns out to be an experience which is at the same time supportive and challenging, enjoyable and painful
  - the reformulation of participants' issues often leads to an unexpected discovery of the positive-within-the-negative and vice versa.
- A growing feeling of being more grounded and less stressed, focusing more on outcomes and self-awareness throughout their leadership process.
- After only nine months, there are clear indications of a strengthening of the BBC's own facilitative function and a heightening of process awareness within both internal consultants and leaders. Action learning is often considered to have played a role in this shift towards 'process consultation'.

It will remain impossible to ascribe outcomes specifically to the action learning initiative, as all participants are having other learning experiences at the same time, in large-group events, workshops, coaching sessions and virtual learning.

Conclusion

With more BBC leaders participating in action learning, we will have a unique opportunity to test a few hypotheses, although we will never be able to obtain definite answers. In a few years time we hope to report on:

- the value of an action learning community, which is an action learning group with no fixed membership
- the effects of this grand-scale action learning initiative on leadership within the BBC, and its relative merits with respect to leadership training and coaching
- new, autonomous initiatives arising from our peer consultation effort with 'maximal freedom' and 'continuous inquiry', if any.

Summary of first evaluations

Respondents describing their experience:	Very positive – 17	77%
	Positive – 5	23%
	Negative – 0	0%
Attendance at all sessions:		77%
Respondents that will be continuing in their sets, self-facilitated:	18	82%
Respondents' feedback on their facilitator's style:	Very positive – 16	73%
	Positive – 5	23%
	Negative – 0	0%

Key learning points (summarised into key themes):

'I'm not alone in having these issues/ the value of sharing' (×14)
'Listening more' (×7)
'Not having to know all the answers' (×6)
'Thinking more' (×3)
'Communicating more clearly'
'Leading teams better/dealing with difficult colleagues'

What you're doing differently (summarised into key themes):

'Letting others work through issues/ not having to know the answer' (×11)
'Using the wider network' (×5)
'Have more confidence' (×5)
'Thinking more' (×3)
'Delegating' (×2)

Comments offered:

'Make it available to all of the BBC!'
'Create a system for people to form new sets if theirs isn't bonding/working well'
'Make it non-optional!'
'Can the BBC help us to organise the sessions, rather than relying on individuals to do them?'
'At end of Leadership Programme get people to put their names down if they want to form new sets going forward'
'Get funding for set meetings (rooms and travel)'
'Create a new name for 'Action Learning'. We were too embarrassed to use it: we just said we were going to a meeting!'
'This must stay as part of the course: it was most useful'

A few direct quotes

'A very powerful tool to help people really address issues that are causing (real and self-imposed) blockages in their working lives. Well facilitated, the set learns how to push the boundaries with each other and with the topics under discussion.'

'In a word – fantastic. I find it really interesting and much more useful than I thought it would be. It's like going to therapy.'

'Specifically, it's helped me hugely with a particular issue I had at work, and the other people in my set have made me feel good about the outcome. More generally, it's so valuable to share things with people who are in completely different areas to my own – they are detached from the politics and characters where I work, and their different perspectives are invaluable. I've also found, to my surprise, that sometimes the best sessions are when I, or others, don't think we have a particular issue, but through the session, something comes out we were almost unaware of (hence the therapy thought).'

'Absolutely invaluable! This method of knowledge sharing and problem solving was one of the big ones in the Ashridge Programme. It has helped me emotionally and practically over the last six months to an enormous degree. Having the ability to share issues and problems in a 'safe' environment, with a group of people who understand the organisation but aren't directly related to the area that one works in, is hugely rewarding.'

'Extremely useful and one of the most productive parts of the Leadership Programme.'

'Action learning has been incredibly valuable, both as a learning tool and as a way of maintaining the momentum of the leadership programme.'

'Our group comprises people of very different personality/leadership types – not people I would have naturally gravitated towards for help, but certainly people who have been able to give me excellent insight into issues. I feel our group works very well together as a learning set but also as a source of general leadership support.'

Bibliography

Anderson, S.L. and Betz, N.E. (2001). Sources of social self-efficacy expectations: their measurement and relation to career development. *Journal of Vocational Behavior* 58, pp. 98–117.

Argyris, C. and Schön, D. (1978). *Organizational Learning: a theory of action perspective.* Reading, Mass: Addison-Wesley.

Armstrong, D. (1997). The 'institution in the mind': reflections on the relation of psycho-analysis to work with institutions. *Free Associations* 41, pp. 1–14.

Armstrong, D. (2003). Keeping on moving. *Free Associations* 53, pp. 1–13.

Asch, S.E. (1951). Effects of group pressure upon the modification and distortion of judgments. In: *Groups, Leadership and Men* (ed. H. Guetzkow), pp. 177–90. Pittsburgh: Carnegie.

Balint, M. (1957). *The Doctor, His Patient and the Illness.* London: Pitman Medical.

Bandura, A. (1982). Self-efficacy mechanism in human agency. *American Psychologist* 37(2), pp. 122–47.

Bateson, G. (1942). Social planning and the concept of deuterolearning. Reprinted (1973) in: *Steps to an Ecology of Mind.* Herts, UK: Paladin.

Bion, W.R. (1961). *Experiences in Groups.* London: Tavistock.

Bion, W.R. (1965). *Transformations.* London: William Heinemann Medical Books.

Boshyk, Y. (ed.) (2000). *Business Driven Action Learning: global best practices.* London and New York: Macmillan Business.

Boshyk, Y. (ed.) (2002). *Action Learning Worldwide: experiences of leadership and organisational development.* Basingstoke, UK: Palgrave Macmillan.

Broad, M.L. and Newstrom, J.W. (1992). *Transfer of Training: action-packed strategies to ensure high payoff from training investments.* Reading, Mass: Addison-Wesley.

Casey, D. (1976). The emerging role of set adviser in action learning programmes. *Journal of European Training* 5(3), pp. 1–14.

Casey, D. and Pearce, D. (eds) (1977). *More than Management Development: action learning at GEC.* Farnborough, UK: Gower.

Casey, D., Roberts, P. and Salaman, G. (1992). Facilitating learning in groups. *Leadership and Organization Development Journal* 13(4), pp. 8–13.

Corno, L. (1986). The metacognitive control components of self-regulated learning. *Contemporary Educational Psychology* 11, pp. 333–46.

Cunningham, I. (1994). *The Wisdom of Strategic Learning: the self managed learning solution.* Maidenhead, UK: McGraw-Hill.

de Haan, E. (1999). Weldadig spreken met dubbele tong: ironie als techniek van de helpende buitenstaander bij veranderingen [Speaking helpfully with a 'double tongue': irony as a technique of the helping outsider in change]. *Filosofie in bedrijf* 34, pp. 54–64.

de Haan, E. (2003). *The Consulting Process as Drama*. London: Karnac.

de Haan, E. and Burger, B. (2004). *Coaching with Colleagues: an action guide to individual consultation*. Basingstoke, UK: Palgrave Macmillan.

de Haan, E. and de Ridder, E. (2003). Intercollegiale consultatie in de praktijk: hoe leren deelnemers? [Action learning in practice: how do participants learn?] *Management & Organisatie* 3, pp. 5–30.

Dewey, J. (1910). *How We Think*. Boston, Mass: Heath.

Dewey, J. (1938). *Experience and Education*. New York: Kappa Delta Pi.

Driehuis, M. (1997). *De Lerende Adviseur: een onderzoek naar intercollegiaal consult in organisatieadvisering* [The learning consultant: research into peer consultation in organisation consulting]. Delft, the Netherlands: Eburon.

Gosling, R., Miller, D.H., Woodhouse, D. and Turquet, P.M. (1967). *The Use of Small Groups in Training*. London: Colmcote.

Grochowiak, K. and Castella, J. (2002). *Systemdynamische Organisationsberatung* [System-dynamic organisation consulting]. Heidelberg, Germany: Carl Auer Systeme Verlag.

Haddon, M. (2003). *The Curious Incident of the Dog in the Night-Time*. London: Random House.

Harrison, R. (1963). Defenses and the need to know. *Human Relations Training News* 6(4), pp. 1–3.

Harrison, R. (1970). Choosing the depth of organizational intervention. *Journal of Applied Behavioral Science* 6(2), pp. 189–202.

Harrison, R. (1995). *Consultant's Journey: a professional and personal odyssey*. Maidenhead, UK: McGraw-Hill.

Honey, P. and Mumford, A. (1986). *Using Your Learning Styles*. Maidenhead, UK: McGraw-Hill.

James, W. (1890). *The Principles of Psychology*. New York: Holt, Rinehart and Winston.

Jennings, D. (2002). Strategic management: an evaluation of the use of three learning methods. *Journal of Management Development* 21(9), pp. 655–65.

Jung, C.G. (1921). *Psychologische Typen*. Olten, Switzerland: Walter-Verlag AG,. Translated as Psychological types in *Collected Works of C.G. Jung*, Volume VI. London: Routledge and Kegan Paul, 1971.

Koenderink, J.J. (1999). Brain scanning and the single mind. *Perception* 28, pp. 1181–4.

Kolb, D.A. (1984). *Experiential Learning: experience as the source of learning and development*. Englewood Cliffs, NJ: Prentice Hall.

Lewin, K. (1951). *Field Theory in Social Sciences*. New York: Harper and Row.

Luft, J. (1969). *Of Human Interaction*. Palo Alto, Calif: Mayfield.

March, J.G. (1991). Exploration and exploitation in organizational learning. *Organization Science* 2, pp. 71–87.

Marquardt, M.J. (1999). *Action Learning in Action*. Palo Alto, Calif: Davies-Black.

Maslow, A.H. (1962). *Toward a Psychology of Being*. Princeton, NJ: Van Nostrand.

McGill, A. and Beaty, L. (1992). *Action Learning: a guide for professional, management and educational development*. London: Kogan Page.

Nonaka, I. and Takeuchi, H. (1995). *The Knowledge Creating Company*. New York: Oxford University Press.

Obholzer, A. and Zagier Roberts, V. (1994). *The Unconscious at Work*. London: Routledge.

Pearce, D. (1983). Getting started: an action manual. In: *Action Learning in Practice* (ed. M. Pedler), pp. 349–66. Aldershot, UK: Gower.

Pedler, M. (ed.) (1983). *Action Learning in Practice*. Aldershot, UK: Gower.

Pedler, M. (1996). *Action Learning for Managers*. London: Lemos and Crane.

Piaget, J. (1970). *Epistémologie génétique*. Paris: Presses Universitaires de France. (Dutch translation: Genetische epistemologie. Meppel, the Netherlands: Boom, 1976.)

Polanyi, M. (1966). *The Tacit Dimension*. New York: Doubleday.

Raguse, B. and Raguse, H. (1980). Ein TZI-Modell der Supervision [A TZI model of supervision]. *Gruppenpsychotherapie und Gruppendynamik* 15, pp. ????????.

Revans, R.W. (1978). *The ABC of Action Learning*. London: Lemos and Crane.

Rogers, C.R. (1957). Personal thoughts on teaching and learning. *Merril-Palmer Quarterly* 3, pp. 241–43. Reprinted in: *On Becoming a Person: a therapist's view of psychotherapy*. London: Constable, 1961.

Rogers, C.R. (1958). A process conception of psychotherapy. *American Psychologist* 13, pp. 142–9. Reprinted in: *On Becoming a Person: a therapist's view of psychotherapy*. London: Constable, 1961.

Russell, B. (1912). *The Problems of Philosophy*. London: Butterworth.

Saks, A.M. (1997). Transfer of training and self-efficacy: what is the dilemma? *Applied Psychology: an international review* 46(4), pp. 365–70.

Schein, E.H. (1987). *Process Consultation*, volume II. Reading, Mass: Addison-Wesley.

Schein, E.H., Schneier, I. and Barker, C.H. (1961). *Coercive Persuasion*. New York: W.W. Norton and Co.

Schön, D. (1983). *The Reflective Practitioner: how professionals think in action*. New York: Basic.

Schön, D. (1987). *Educating the Reflective Practitioner*. San Francisco: Jossey-Bass.

Schutz, W.C. (1958). *FIRO: a three-dimensional theory of interpersonal behaviour*. New York: Rinehart.

Shaw, P. (2002). *Changing Conversations in Organisations: a complexity approach to change*. London and New York: Routledge.

Sherer, M. and Maddux, J.E. (1982). The self-efficacy scale: construction and validation. *Psychological Reports* 51, pp. 663–71.

Schroder, M. (1974). The shadow consultant. *Journal of Applied Behavioral Science* 10(4), pp. 579–94.

Simons, P.R.J. (2000). Towards a constructivistic theory of self-directed learning. In: *Self-Learning* (ed. G. Straka). Berlin: Waxman.

Teeuw, B., Schwarzer, R. and Jerusalem, M. (1994). *Dutch Adaptation of the General Self-Efficacy Scale*. http://userpage.fu-berlin.de/~health/dutch.htm.

van der Krogt, F.J. (1998). Learning network theory: the tension between learning systems and work systems in organizations. *Human Resource Development Quarterly* 9(2), pp. 157–78.

Watzlawick, P., Beavin, J. and Jackson, D.D. (1967). *Pragmatics of Human Communication*. New York: W.W. Norton.

Weick, K.E. and Westley, F. (1996). Organizational learning: affirming an oxymoron.

In: *Handbook of Organization Studies* (ed. S.R. Clegg, C. Hardy and W.R. Nord), pp. 440–58. London: Sage.

Weinstein, K. (1995). *Action Learning: a journey in discovery and development.* London: HarperCollins.

Weinstein, K. (2002). Action learning: the classic approach. In: *Action Learning Worldwide: experiences of leadership and organisational development* (ed. Y. Boshyk), pp. 3–18. Basingstoke, UK: Palgrave Macmillan.

Wiener, N. (1948). *Cybernetics.* New York: John Wiley.

Index